Letting Off
STEAM

The Railway Paintings of

David Weston

First published in Great Britain in 2009

British Library Cataloguing-in-Publication Data
A CIP record for this title is available from the British Library

ISBN 978 1 906690 08 3

HALSGROVE
Halsgrove House,
Ryelands Industrial Estate,
Bagley Road, Wellington, Somerset TA21 9PZ
Tel: 01823 653777   Fax: 01823 216796
email: sales@halsgrove.com

Part of the Halsgrove group of companies
Information on all Halsgrove titles is available at: www.halsgrove.com

Printed and bound by Grafiche Flaminia, Italy

Contents

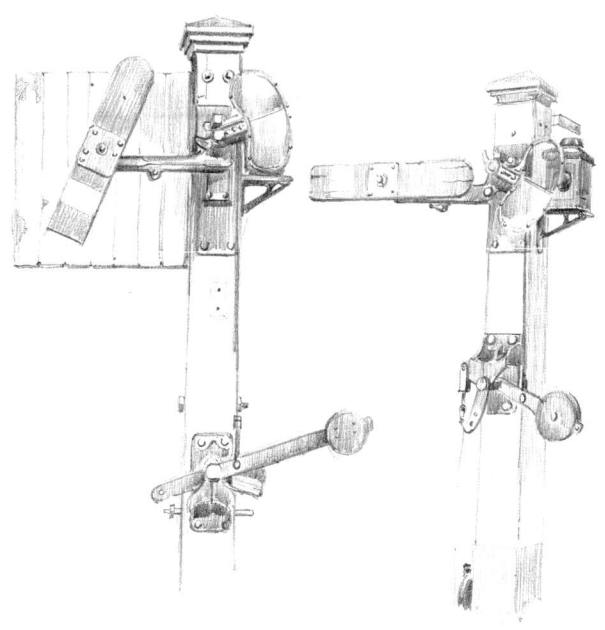

For Karen with much love

Acknowledgements

I am enormously grateful to Simon Butler, my publisher, for his enthusiasm over the publication of this, my third book for Halsgrove.
To Sharon O'Inn and Denise Lyons I owe a big thank you for their part in its production, and indeed to all the staff at
Halsgrove for their continuing support.

My daughter Karen has once again managed to make sense of my handwritten text and done
her stalwart work on the computer prior to handing the manuscript over.

For his most generous and enthusiastic foreword I am greatly indebted to Paul Atterbury. His enthusiasm for
my work is very much appreciated and his knowledge of both art and railways is well known through his
many books and his frequent appearances on the BBC's Antiques Roadshow.

For much of the photographic work of the paintings and of the railway layout I must thank Andrew Pennill LRPS,
for his care and expertise, and to Roger Brooks for his part in supplying copies of those paintings reproduced as fine art prints.

To the owners of the paintings reproduced here I must offer a huge thank you, not only for buying
them in the first place but also for not objecting to their inclusion in this book.

And finally, as always, my sincere appreciation to my wife Mary who has to cope with me
whilst I am engaged on these projects. And believe me, that's not easy!

Foreword
by Paul Atterbury

Watercolour is the great English painting medium and, since its popular development at the end of the eighteenth century, it has been associated with a litany of famous names including Cozens, Girtin, Sandby, Cotman, Constable, Turner, De Wint, Cox and Ruskin. Most of these were landscape painters, responding directly to the picturesque appeal of the British countryside with its particular mixture of raw nature and the enduring impact of the hand of man, past and present. In the early nineteenth century a watercolourist would paint with equal facility wild mountains, hills and river valleys, the domestic landscape, ancient ruins and architecture and the monuments of modern industry, such as a canal aqueduct or lock, or even an ironworks.

In the Victorian period the romantic watercolour vision of the landscape continued to flourish but in the early years of the twentieth century it died away, devastated by the impact of modernism, only to be revived from the 1930s by artists such as Paul Nash and Eric Ravilious, and later by John Piper and Edward Seago. David Weston is an artist firmly in this British watercolour tradition but he has carried forward the baton of romantic painting into the twenty-first century. He works in watercolours and oils but is primarily a watercolourist and a master of the complex and demanding techniques of this craft. He carries, therefore, lightly and instinctively the inevitable stamp of his great predecessors, from Cotman to Piper. He is aware of his debt to the past but is clearly a contemporary artist with echoes of modern masters such as the great American watercolourist, Andrew Wyeth, and a painter with no fear of abstraction. He has been there and knows well that in British painting the primary inspiration for abstraction has always been the landscape.

Weston has been a professional artist for over forty years and his subject matter is correspondingly diverse. He loves the British landscape and its history but his favourite subjects come from industry and the railways, subjects, albeit in decline, that surrounded him as he grew up. He paints what he has seen, returning constantly for inspiration to the sketchbooks and drawings of his early life. As a result, decay and dereliction figure strongly in paintings whose inspiration is the end of an era in British industrial history.

Opposite page:
Winston Churchill,
oil painting, size 18"x 24"

He lived through and drew the decline of railways, mining, iron production and heavy engineering. This sets him apart from many of his contemporaries working in this field who paint retrospectively to create highly coloured fantasy visions of an imaginary and idealised past. By contrast, his images of industrial dereliction and decay, shadowy components of a lost world, echo in their controlled and deliberately limited palette the romanticism of Piper in his paintings of bombed cities and shattered architecture. In the same way, he has a concern for accuracy and detail that he does not allow to dominate the work in the pedantic way of many modern railway artists. More important is the concern for composition, colour and technique that allows him to blend the precise observation contained in a sketch made four decades ago with a painterly approach to atmosphere and light. He has this in common with his hero and mentor, Terence Cuneo, another great railway artist who painted the present as he saw it, not the past as he imagined it.

This book concentrates on railway paintings and the selection, in watercolour and oil, enables David Weston to revisit the railway history of his own life. The images are evocative and highly romantic, in the painterly meaning of the word. Their subjects cross the railway spectrum, from little industrial locomotives abandoned in remote sheds to the last generation of main line giants, all captured in that last glorious decade of British steam. It is a vision of a lost world but it is the real thing, not the painstaking recreation of the preserved railway, and the retrospective railway painter. Atmosphere, a particular feeling for colour sensibility and realism dominate, and link the paintings together, along with Weston's consummate skill as an artist.

David Weston in his studio.

Not So Much An Introduction

More A Way of Life

"Ay-up, are you David Weston?" I was in the picture-framers on a bleak Monday morning and with a howler of a headache. Grudgingly, I acknowledged with a nod that I was. "I thought you were, I thought you were." His voice filled the shop and reverberated through my aching brain. "Now then, I bought one of your prints yesterday." "Oh," I said, half-heartedly. And then curiosity took a hold. "So where did you buy that then, on a Sunday?" "Oh, a car boot." "Ah," I said, "and how much did you pay for it?" Of course, I should have stopped digging by then but such is life – one seldom learns. "I gave 50p for it." Crestfallen further I replied that he had done rather well at that. "Ah well..." he continued with a pause, "You can have it back if you like. I only bought it for the frame!"

I have suffered quite a few put-downs and knock-backs in my career as an artist over the years but a triple whammy on a Monday morning when I was not at my best remains etched in my memory on these matters, and is a constant reminder that an essential ingredient for a life as an artist is a good sense of humour.

To put a little perspective on just who I am as an artist I should perhaps explain that the railway scene is only one aspect of my overall inspiration for painting pictures. The natural extension to this is a fascination for industrial landscapes with or without railways, and then in complete contrast is my enthusiasm to paint the natural landscape of both the British Isles and Continental Europe, together with the rich diversity of their architecture.

Architecture and interior subjects feature largely in my yearly production of paintings, as does transport of all descriptions from motor cars to ships at sea. So my living as a painter through the later half of the twentieth century and now into the twenty-first has been derived from being somewhat of an all-rounder rather than purely as a painter of railways, and I have indeed been well-blessed in that respect.

My enthusiasm for railways and in particular the steam era has been constant since early childhood. Born in 1935 I can well remember as a boy seeing immaculate apple-green A3s and those amazing garter-blue A4s at Grantham. Then in complete contrast were the war-blackened streamlined Coronations rattling at high speed through a vibrating Nuneaton station.

So my interest goes back a long way and as a Leicestershire lad it is only natural, I suppose, to be swayed ever since towards the engines and atmosphere of the Midland and North-Eastern regions rather than those of the counties further South whose delights I only discovered in later years.

Most railway enthusiasts I guess were at one time trainspotters. Oh yes, that dreadful title, much maligned these days and often the subject of ridicule. But of course that is where my interest began, an interest that would some two-and-a-half decades later lead me to become the professional painter I so longed to be. Looking back briefly to those days of standing on draughty station platforms or sneaking around locomotive sheds with a thumping heart, my Ian Allen log-book held tightly in my hand, it would have been inconceivable to me then that this boyhood fascination with steam engines could lead in later life to the achievement of an ambition to become a professional artist. But there can be no doubt at all that had I not maintained that interest in railways and come in time to paint them, then I very much doubt that I may never have made it as a full-time artist, because it was indeed the paintings of the steam era that eventually led me to a prestigious London showing and the consequent opportunity to paint professionally.

A little of that story will doubtless be reflected within the text of this book but I must be careful as so much has been covered of this aspect of my career in *For the Love of Steam*, published by David & Charles, and the earlier book *Beware of Trains* by Ian Allen.

Although the first railway painting I ever did was in 1953 it would have been towards 1965 that I started to paint railways with some regularity. My wife Mary and I had a small drapery shop at that time and fortunately it was right next to the main London–Midland line to the North coming out of Leicester.

Parting the underwear and towels hanging in the shop window I would see with increasing regularity, lines of sad locomotives being towed by on their way to the scrapyards and the cutter's torch. It was indeed a wake-up call and I decided to get out and about to record as much as I could before it was just too late. What I did was not enough by any means and how I wish now I had spent far more time with my sketchbook and paints in the engine yards and sheds that were so rapidly changing or, even worse, disappearing completely from town and country alike.

As an artist painting such subject matter it seemed at the time to be a bit unusual. Certainly none of my many artist friends in the Leicester Society of Artists had any interest in the subject, and most told me it was a total waste of time. But I just loved painting steam engines – not with any ambition at all for display. In fact the thought of an exhibition of such work never entered my head. It was a private thing, done purely for pleasure.

So I felt very much a loner at that time and of course there were no associations in those days such as the Guild of Railway Artists which only came along much later, in 1979. They, and the artists that comprise its membership have done much over the years to further the status of railway art and their exhibitions display a considerable variety of techniques in various media.

Back in the late 1960s it would have been incredibly rare to have seen a railway painting included in an art exhibition and certainly the London art scene generally viewed such paintings with absolute disdain. One little story illustrates just what I mean.

Through 1967 and '68 I was humping my paintings around the London galleries trying desperately to find someone to take me up and represent my work. In the portfolio were traditional paintings of architectural subjects, landscapes, and just the odd one or two steam engine pictures. My landscapes etc. were dismissed as too ordinary and the railway paintings as of no account whatsoever. A typical comment was that steam engines were on their way out and no one was interested in them! How short-sighted was that?

It was brought home to me one day, when being thrown out of the umpteenth gallery, when the owner said as I reached the door, "Hey, you know what it says on the railway on those cast-iron signs? It says 'Beware of Trains' - I should if I were you." Coming back home to Leicester on the train that night that comment haunted my thoughts and I vowed that if I ever made it as a professional artist and railways had anything to do with it, then one of those signs would be fixed to the wall of my future studio, and I am proud to say that within just three years of that farewell comment being tossed at me I was doing just that – and it is there to this day. Incidentally, that also gave me the title for that first book of my railway paintings and also the ATV documentary film about my life, which fortunately coincided with its publication.

A glance at the paintings in this book will show a difference of technique between those painted in oils and ones where watercolour has been the chosen medium. I have never been drawn to paint in anything like a photographic manner where every bit of gravel on the track is accounted for and fully explained. I cannot really see the point when a cracking good photograph does the same. This does not detract from the ability and polished technique of those who do, it is all a matter of taste at the end of the day. But I really feel that the viewing of a painting should be a two-way experience, the viewer contributing through the evocation of memories and their own experience. If the artist leaves a little unsaid it gives room for such an interaction to take place.

A looser technique in both the media I have enjoyed over the years is the path I have followed, and it is what has come naturally to me. An artist's technique is something that is developed over time and should be a true expression of the painter's personality. To be true to oneself is essential for interpretation beyond the earlier stages of learning how to paint.

Both media are fascinating to produce. With oils the paint has to be pushed around – it does not move otherwise. Whereas with watercolour the paint runs constantly and can easily go out of control unless a tight rein is kept on its progression, particularly when working on wet paper! From this it may be no surprise when I say that I find watercolour to be the most difficult of all media, but certainly it is the most fascinating and rewarding to produce.

Some of the paintings in this medium that are reproduced within the following pages also have the addition of a pen line. This is sometimes referred to as line and wash. The drawing of the scene is generally done first where a pen line is used either in black or brown ink and before any colour is put on to the paper. Whatever happens thereafter with the application of washes, that line will remain constant as an important part of the construction of the painting and its perceived technique, so contributing strongly to the finished effect.

There are several examples in the book of this method and it is a way of interpretation that I love. I find it very conducive to creating atmosphere in the scene, and of course atmosphere is something that I consider to be absolutely paramount to the success of any painting.

Atmosphere, light, and interesting colour are my number one aims when constructing a painting. Drawing is also very important to get right and is always a top priority in putting a composition together. There is much to think about in painting a picture, so many pitfalls – particularly so with the railway scene where authenticity plays such an important role. One can bend a tree or move a post, but it is rather more difficult to play about too much with a locomotive!

It is a little over twenty years now since the last book of my railway work was published (*For The Love of Steam*, 1988) and I have felt over that time that I would not want to produce another book about my railway paintings. However, more recently it occurred to me that the three already published only show the work produced up to the 1980s and as I have done a great deal since then – many more in recent years, using the medium of watercolour in addition to oils, then a new book inclusive of these later works may not be inappropriate.

So how could I make this volume a little different and something more than just another selection of railway pictures? I thought it may be interesting to invite the reader into the studio, and to enjoy through a few photographs the atmosphere of the place together with some of the railway-related objects that evoke memories and reflect that part of my artistic life.

Within a yard or two of the easel for instance is my industrial railway layout, which recreates in model form the ironstone workings of the East Midlands – something that also features in the paintings reproduced later in this book on that particular aspect of the railway field. And then there are memories – lots of those – of men and machines and people who have come along through the course of my long career to colour my life, and often to have formed friendships which one treasures so much.

I hope the reader will enjoy this peep into my painting life. Included in the paintings will be just a small selection from the 1970s and 80s – not many, but a few that represent those years, and of course many new ones that have not been published before that will illustrate the paintings of the ensuing years almost to the present day.

Loughborough Central Station
Gt Central Railway.
12·7·2003.

9F on Freight, oil painting, size 18"x 24"

Busy Day at the Junction, oil painting, size 20"x 30"

St Helen's Junction in Lancashire is the setting for this painting done in 2004 for my friend and collector, Joe Spencer. The time is the late 1950s with Jubilee class engine No 45581 'Bihar and Orissa' heading towards Earlstown, and 'Jinty' No 47393 waiting to round the curve to Sutton Oak.

There was much to include in this commissioned piece to satisfy Joe's memory of the scene as he knew it, and indeed as he had travelled to and fro many times on the footplate of the 'Jinty'.

Burton Agness Hall at Didcot, oil painting, size 16"x 20"

Last Links With Tilton, oil painting, size 10"x 14"

A small oil with a lot of atmosphere. The story the painting has to tell is that of a wet day, a lonely station and the last train to ever stop there – and perhaps the despondency of the figures about to leave the station for the last time.

The original of this painting has ended up a long way from home with one of my clients in California, an unlikely subject to find on a wall in America perhaps, but Debbie Ruth has a great feeling for the iron horse and has a 'Weston' room in her house for my pictures. I am indebted to her for its inclusion in this book.

The Box for Sleaford Junction, oil painting size 10"x 14"

A back street in Boston beside the railway, typical of many throughout the country, but it made a dramatic statement about such areas that proved irresistible for me to express in this small oil painting.

Britannia at Crewe, oil painting, size 30"x 40"

Princess in the Snow, oil painting, size 30"x 40"

Oil Cans in the Shed, watercolour size 7.25"x 6.75"

The textures of the oily surfaces of these cans was what attracted me to this low eye-level interpretation of the subject. That and the dramatic contrast between the strong light on the oil cans and the almost black background with just a hint of a workbench to the left hand top corner.

Southern Power, oil painting, size 18"x 24"

Merchant Navy Class No 35005 Canadian Pacific on shed.

Sunlight in the Shed, oil painting, size 20"x 24"

This is one of several paintings I have produced over the years of Holbeck shed. Of all the Midland sheds Holbeck held a special magic in its ability on a sunny day to weave a wonderful tapestry of fleeting sunrays combined with steam and smoke.

Even the most massive engine could be transformed to an ethereal image of broken masses and glinting highlights. The engine here is one of my favourite Jubilee class No 45618 'New Hebrides' in its state of faded livery, dirt and grime. The whole scene creates an evocative picture of steam towards the end of the era – working engines in a real workaday setting.

The Power and the Princess, oil painting, size 30"x 40"

The amazing light and shade of the cuttings at Liverpool provide the setting for this commissioned painting of 'Princess Margaret Rose' for the locomotive's owner Brell Ewart. Brell wanted a powerful and dramatic image of his engine in its green livery during its BR days.

The large-sized canvas gave me full scope to capture the intense sunlight and depth of shadow that this location was renowned for.

Heavy Freight for Tyne Docks, watercolour, size 13"x 19"

Quenching the Thirst, watercolour, size 9"x 12"

This is a very loose and fluid use of watercolour for such a complicated subject and of course the light in the picture is of the utmost importance to get right. Back-lit scenes hold many pitfalls for an artist as there is always the tendency to overstate the contrasts involved. I loved the reflected lights on the engine and I was very careful not to overdo the strength of colour on the water tank so it did not conflict with the rear of the engine, which had to be the strongest dark. The group of figures watching the procedure of quenching the engine's thirst for water make the picture, once again simple in treatment so as not to detract from the main elements of the locomotive and its crew.

England Their England

A snapshot of a '40s boyhood

If there was one thing you could never ever do on a bicycle it was to ride the tramlines. More than once my wheels accidentally slipped into them and off I came. There was no avoiding it, especially so on a wet day.

Only once did I see it done as I waited in Leicester's Belgrave Gate for the tram home. From out of a public house opposite came a staggering drunk, trying desperately to wheel his bike into the middle of the road. The queue of some thirty or forty people watched with mounting amusement as his weaving progress turned to pure slapstick comedy as he tried repeatedly to get his leg over the crossbar and himself on to the saddle. With the tram queue by then in a state of near hysteria our star turn quite suddenly achieved his goal and proceeded to ride off along the tramline to a rousing cheer, as straight as a die and into the distance.

If he had been able to keep on going long enough he would have arrived at Melton Turn, a sort of high spot on routes one and two for the tramcars. It was the bustling junction where route one veered off to Belgrave and trams bearing route number two carried on towards the Melton Road terminus.

I liked Melton Turn as a boy in the 1930s and '40s. It was an exciting spot. On the one side of the road was Bacon's Garage, a rambling old building where Pole's Luxury Coaches in their smart black and white livery vied for my attention with a fascinating array of petrol pumps offering the motorist a choice of Shell, Dominion or Carless fuel. Who thought that name up!? On the other side of the road, amongst an incredibly varied number of shops, was North's Travel Agency and Toy Shop where the window always displayed a veritable feast of Dinky Toys whose bright colours echoed in miniature the very liveries of the vehicles that passed by outside. Nothing, it seemed, had been missed to set a young boy's pulses racing, from a dark green Atco Mowers van to one of my favourites, the black and red Royal Mail van complete with its gold GR emblem and crown emblazoned on its sides. The choice was endless and I wanted them all. Even the military vehicles I was coming to see with increasing regularity on the streets were there in model form. I remember looking longingly at the searchlight lorry with its massive light pointing skywards, and the Royal Tank Corps set in its bright blue box that was always well beyond the pockets of my beleaguered parents.

Mr Frank Hornby, the Liverpool entrepreneur, had seen to it that a boy of my generation was not without plenty to interest and educate him. Not only had he given us the much revered Dinky Toys but our hobby needs were further catered for by Meccano construction kits, and of course the wonderful tin plate train sets that carried his name.

The greatest thing was to have an electric train set and somehow one Christmas my parents managed to buy me a simple boxed set that consisted of an LMS 0.4.0. tank engine with a couple of coaches and a circle of track. Over time as money would allow this was expanded on to include a selection of wagons, a signal box and station, some signals and an engine shed with more track.

Hornby tin plate wagons.

I was a lucky chap to have such a train set in those years of the early '40s, but it was before the effects of the war with Germany made expenditure of that sort on such a luxury would become totally prohibitive. Miraculously Hornby's greatest achievement in terms of their model engine manufacture came in 1937 with the production of the LMS Princess Elizabeth locomotive in its magnificent shining maroon livery with yellow lining and chromium handrails and fittings. It was far more than I dare aspire to at one-hundred-and-fifty shillings, a considerable sum then for a toy, and one that only the well-off might afford.

What Hornbys produced were far from scale models but each item, be it a wagon, engine or building, had great colour and a special character that is a delight to this day, and still avidly collected. There are a few reminders in my studio to recall those boyhood years; a green LNER tank engine with a string of colourful trucks, amongst them an eye-catching yellow Portland Cement wagon and the bright red Royal Daylight oil carrier.

With the onset of war in 1939 Hornby's were forced into limiting their production of toys and eventually the Liverpool factories were given over entirely to war work, making everything from bomb release units to hypodermic needles. It was a gradual slide throughout the country into a greyer existence for the best part of the next eight years at least, and it was only the Queen's wedding in 1947 that eventually injected some of the old colour and excitement back into an England that was still suffering from all the austerities of the war years.

We were lucky in a way living where we did in Leicester which was not too badly affected by bombing raids, although as a boy living through those years one had come to accept food rationing and make-do-and-mend clothing because that's how it was. The mad dash up the garden to the Anderson shelter in the dark of night was exciting to a boy whose understanding of what was really happening was limited. The mournful wail of the warning siren set dread into my parents' hearts but joy into mine because I just loved sleeping in a bunk in the cosy but dimly lit interior of the corrugated iron retreat which my father had wallpapered but which was always damp and fusty with a smell that was a mixture of that and candle fat. For safety we were able to buy nightlights which did the same job but were only a couple of inches high and twice as thick as a normal candle.

Within a few years the old shelter had been taken down and traffic in the streets had returned to normal. The military convoys had disappeared and once again Pat Collin's great showman's engines trundled their colourful loads to the October fair. And what a delight that was, wedged as it was on a patch of bare ground beside St Mark's Church and the old gas works, from which steam lorries carrying coke emerged at regular intervals to spit their red hot cinders on to the tramlines.

The fair was fascinating, not so much to me for the rides but for the massive engines that drove them. There, at the back of all the light and glitz these great monsters rocked rhythmically on their chocks. Brilliantly lit from beneath their canopies great fly-wheels propelled their flapping belts amid a cacophony of hissing sounds. To a small boy it was totally captivating, a different world of colour and excitement further enhanced by the discovery of the showman's living wagons. These beautifully decorated caravans drew my interest

Nightlights.

The showman's wagon at the Lazyacre.

considerably and a glimpse inside their lush interiors was enough to glue me to the spot until told by an irate occupant to clear off!

Here, within their confined and compact living space, the showman displayed his finest Crown Derby and Worcester porcelain. It was reflected in mirror-fronted mahogany cupboards, softly lit by the light of two or three ruby oil lamps. The mystery and delight of those boyhood glimpses into the fairground's living quarters remained with me over the years, until in 1970 I was able to purchase a lovely old showman's wagon to restore and care for. Built originally by Orton and Spooner in Burton-upon-Trent during 1900 it now remains resplendent and complete in our garden at The Lazy Acre, sixty years on at least from those days of the post-war October fairs.

As the decade of the 1940s drew to its rambling close the steam lorries from the gas works no longer dropped their ash and sparks on to the tramlines (not by then that there were many left in Leicester to suffer the indignity). The last tram to run on Leicester's lines was in November 1949. The City decided in its wisdom to uproot the tracks and tear down some of the best of the architectural features that for decades had made it utterly different to anywhere else. A portent of the future I did not fully grasp at the time.

A page from my Ian Allen stock book.

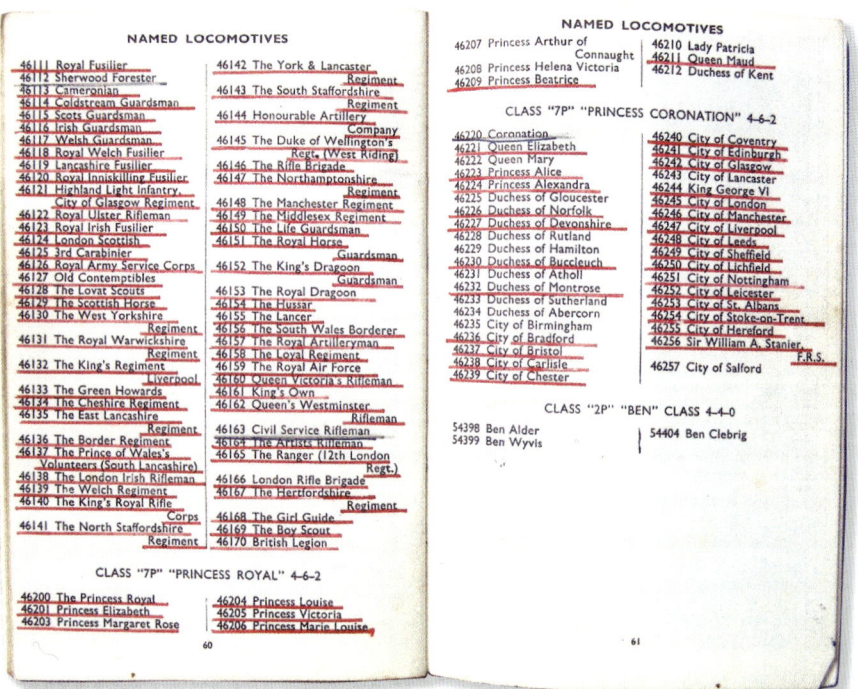

The tramcars had taken me to school each day and although we were persuaded that the new buses were far more comfortable they certainly were nowhere near as exciting. To ride on the upper deck in the front cabin with the sliding door shut to the rest of the tram was the best. From there one could see everything and fully experience the swaying and rocking that was so thrilling when the driver let rip on the controls. And in concurrence with the bold notice of 'NO SPITTING' Leicester's trams were always immaculate. Their livery was elegant in a rich maroon and cream, set off on a lower panel with the legend 'Leicester City Tramways' in gold-shaded lettering with the civic crest above spelling out the Latin 'Semper Eadem' which means 'always the same'. Well, they got that one wrong.

The 1950s saw a gradual change in the England I had known as a boy and a very different one indeed from my parents' point of view. The Festival of Britain in 1951 heralded a bright new future promising a better life for all, and indeed the 1950s did revive much of the colour and character that had made a pre-war Britain so very different to anywhere else in the world.

But change and the desire to modernise was in the air, and not only in our towns and cities. The railways that formed such a vast network in connecting them were also in transition. The big four companies became amalgamated under the powers of the Transport Act on 1st January 1948, becoming British Railways. The old individual liveries of the separate companies slowly disappeared and new powerful locomotives were being designed and built under the new regime.

As a teenager in the 1950s I was witnessing many changes in all spheres of life and was becoming rapidly aware that so much of what I had grown up with and loved was disappearing fast. The face of England, my England, and that of my parents a generation earlier was changing forever, and not always by any means for the better. But more of that later.

So this was the background that formed my interest in all forms of transport and led to the desire to paint it. The excitement as a boy of collecting motor car names, and there was a great variety of both British and foreign cars on the roads then and indeed right through to the '50s, was only one aspect of a boyhood mania for collecting such things, including bus types and company names, and of course locomotive numbers, and best of all locomotive names. What a thrill it was for a youngster to see a 'namer' that had not been seen before, and the unrivalled pleasure of underlining it in red ink in my Ian Allen stock book.

No wonder I grew up wanting to make pictures of such things!

Sir Hugo, oil painting, size 24"x 36"

This is a memory of my days at Grantham as a boy watching these beautiful apple-green A3 locomotives with their rakes of teak coaches – a most splendid sight. I chose 'Sir Hugo' for this painting because Hugo is also the name of my grandson and of course I well remember once seeing the locomotive above, looking just as immaculate as it does in the painting. I chose also to paint the engine with the old LNER numbering within the setting of Grantham station prior to the later removal of the magnificent semaphore signals near to the yard box.

Despite this painting being of the more colourful and perhaps glamorised vision of the glory years of British steam I have tried to inject a sense of drama into it as the engine begins its journey south, and as much atmosphere as possible through the lighting of the composition. It is a recreation of the many vivid memories from my boyhood years, and as such is rather personal I suppose, but I hope it will ring a bell with many more who also can recall those years of mid twentieth-century steam.

The Yards at Leicester, watercolour, size 15"x 22"

This large watercolour of a corner of Leicester's Midland Yard gave expression to a long-held desire to produce a painting of this scene as I knew it from boyhood – the lines to the right heading towards the turntable in the very top corner overlooked by the backyards and houses above.

I chose watercolour as the medium for this subject because I wanted a freedom of line and a broad approach which I feel well suits this wet and atmospheric scene. So often I stood in this yard feverishly sketching the scene before me with a wary eye on the movement of locomotives and often, as the picture will suggest, with my sketchbook soaked to the point where drawing would become impossible. No 45682 'Trafalgar', the focal point of this painting, was a frequent visitor to Leicester during those halcyon days of the great steam age.

Sundown, oil painting, size 10"x 14"

Steam at Top Shed, oil painting, size 20"x 30"

Top Shed – Kings Cross, London, in the heyday of the steam years.

Duchess of Sutherland, oil painting, size 16"x 20"

What a magnificent sight the Coronation Pacifics were when working hard and climbing the very backbone of England. The sound of the exhaust echoing across the wild fells of Northumbria, and from a pictorial point of view the contrasts of a polished red engine and its train, with the greens, blues and ochres of nature, would surely inspire any artist, railway enthusiast or not, to take up their brushes.

Evening Departure, oil painting, size 18"x 24"

An unrebuilt Scot leaves a city station with a late departure for the North. It makes a picture of intense darks and many reflected highlights, both on the tracks and of course along the length of the engine itself. Night scenes are always a challenge to paint and my observations and experiences of my younger years when I painted outside at night have often held me in good stead over the years sine.

In those days the best I could manage to help me to see what I was doing was a bicycle lamp on a flexible stem attached to the top of my drawing board - sometimes assisted by a street lamp if I was lucky. The canal in Leicester and the railway yards were a favourite venue at night. Unfortunately all the paintings I did of the railway at night in the 1950s and 60s were torn up in one of my despondent clear-out sessions years ago. A shame, because I could have used what material they offered now, with the benefit of the experience of the years since they were produced.

Steam at Didcot, oil painting, size 16"x 20"

Jubilee, oil painting, size 12"x 16"

Carlisle Citadel, oil painting, size 24"x 36"

This is a painting from 1978, commissioned by the late Rex Blaker who became an avid collector of my railway pictures over many years.

What a stirring sight these most majestic of all Sir William Stanier's locomotives made as they departed from a city station, throwing their huge exhaust into the sky. The threat of heavy weather hangs over Carlisle Citadel in this painting portraying No 6253 'City of St Albans' sometime in the fifties. The engine was built in 1944 at a cost of £15,460 and ran until 1963 covering well over a million miles in the process. Of all Sir William Stanier's engines, these Coronation Pacifics were my favourites. Their line and aesthetic appeal was more than a match for their power and speed. For this study of Carlisle during the 1950s careful research was necessary, including the scrutiny of many photographs of the period.

After Rex died I bought back a number of his originals including 'Carlisle Citadel' and was tempted to keep it for myself, but the inevitable happened and it was sold on. One day perhaps I shall have one of my oils at home. At the time of writing, other than those for my next exhibition, I do not own one.

Silver Link at York, oil painting, size 24"x 30"

Silver Link in its garter blue livery is seen arriving at York in the spring of 1947. That was the specific instruction for this commissioned work executed in 1986. The station at York makes a wonderful frame to the engine and train with the strong sunlight crossing the platform and catching those elegant columns that are such a part of the handsome architecture of this station.

Green Arrow, oil painting, size 20"x 30"

Speed, smoke and sunshine are the key elements in this 1977 painting of Green Arrow.

The London and North Eastern railway under the leadership of Sir Nigel Gresley produced these fine mixed-traffic locomotives from 1936 onwards. Seen here in its original LNER livery I have depicted the locomotive bursting out of Hadley Wood tunnel into the sunshine of a summer's day, the greens of the countryside harmonising with the apple green of the engine to give a unity of colour throughout the painting.

Into the Light, Loughborough,
watercolour, size 15"x 12"

The light on the tracks and the general clutter of old sheds, signals, carriages and water tower was what made this view on the approaches to the station at Loughborough so compelling.

The textures and strength of colour in the foreground, with the light bouncing off those sleepers, draws the eye into the composition and makes a fascinating subject of pure railway atmosphere.

Pensioned Off, oil painting, size 16"x 20"

In this atmospheric scene at Grantham in the last weeks of steam operation I wanted to portray a sadness not just about steam traction but about the men whose working lives had been given to it. They were either facing change or retirement, and many could not face life within the cab of a diesel locomotive. The forlorn appearance of the engine at Grantham in those latter years was in some respects depressing and so different to the well-cared-for engines of my boyhood trainspotting days. But as an artist such scenes inspire me to paint. Those lines of dirty and even rusty engines tell quite a story and make paintings full of pathos and atmosphere. The distant glow in this picture, however, gives a glimmer of hope as it spreads forwards on to the A3 class engine, making a blend of pale yellows and mauves as the light bounces off the boiler and smoke deflector of No 60066 'Merry Hampton'.

Standard Class 4's on Shed, oil painting, size 20"x 24"

The magical effects of light in many steam sheds was always a great motivation to paint. Beams of sunlight and deep shadows crossing the locomotives, combined with those sudden dramatic highlights, was inspiring stuff. This painting of two contrasting Class 4 locomotives, the one behind rather dirty and its neighbour smart in its British Railways green livery, emphasises the sense of drama within a steam shed on a sunny day.

High Drama at Woodhead, oil painting, size 20"x 30"

There can be few more dramatic settings, to see a locomotive thrusting its exhaust skywards after bursting out of a tunnel mouth, than that at Woodhead on the old Great Central line.

The Engine No 60847 of Gresley's V2 class was named 'St Peters School, York AD 627' and was one of only eight of the V2 class that carried a name. They were built between 1936 and 1944 and ran until the end of the steam era, being used for both freight and passenger haulage.

I well remember as a boy sitting on the fence by the line-side watching these engines on the Great Central – I still called it that though of course by then the line had become part of the LNER network. The V2s were regular engines in those days although it was a rarity indeed to see a named one – an occurrence which was greeted by a great chorus of cheers from young enthusiasts that were forever beside the line.

Sunlight on the Talyllyn Railway, oil painting, size 20"x 24"

This painting produced in 1977 shows the scene at Dolgoch station as the engine 'Talyllyn', built in 1865, draws in to pick up passengers on the preserved line between Towyn and Abergynolwyn in North Wales.

The story of the Talyllyn railway in preservation terms goes back to 1949 when a letter appeared in the Birmingham Post about the difficulties of keeping the little narrow-gauge line running. The outcome was the formation of the Talyllyn Railway Preservation Society. It was the first time a group of enthusiasts had ever come together to manage and operate a working railway. No one could ever have imagined then in that group's small beginnings what would happen in future years for the growth of the railway preservation movement, and the consequent number of successful railway lines that now operate countrywide.

Steaming Out of Lincoln, oil painting, size 18"x 24"

The industrial background to this painting might be anywhere within the British railway system, but the cathedral catching the light in the far distance is a dead giveaway, pinpointing the location beyond doubt. Painted in 2006 it epitomizes all my memories of steam in this great city. The B1 class engine, black and grimy, gets away, throwing its exhaust skywards to add to the atmosphere of the general scene. It was a painting I had wanted to do for a long time. My memories of Lincoln, both railway-wise and within the city for painting go back to March 1953 when I practically froze solid painting barges by Brayford Pool. I spent three days battling against frozen paint water! I recall we used to have little tablets that could be put into a tin lid and lit so that the artist could waft the paper over it to dry. The trouble was that if one lingered too long the paper would scorch, or even worse. I remember on one occasion during those three days I burnt a large hole in a nearly completed picture! Such is the life of the all-weather artist.

Night Arrival, oil painting, size 24"x 30"

There was always something very exciting about the arrival of a steam locomotive and its train in the station. It had come from heaven knows where to the familiar accompaniment of echoing station announcements, slamming carriage doors, running feet, trundling mail barrows, shouting voices and the sighs and gurglings of a steam machine whose work was done.

Here the huge bulk of the locomotive reflected along its side a myriad of lights and colours that imbued its form with a certain unfamiliarity and mystery, enhancing its normal daylight appearance.

A Portrait of Power, oil painting, size 30"x 40"

This large oil painting shows one of the magnificent Beyer Garratt locomotives designed by the LMS which were like two engines but with a single boiler fired by coal from a rotary bunker. The engine is hauling the usual coal run from Toton to Brent that these massive locomotives were most suited to. It was a painting that I felt I needed the atmosphere of a wet day and a limited palette colourwise to portray that sense of weight and power in the locomotive.

Black 5 Power, oil painting, size 12"x 16"

Atmosphere and light are, for me, the most important factors in recreating the railway scene that has faded into history. Of course it is of considerable importance to paint the facts correctly – the details of the engine, the setting, or whatever – but this picture illustrates, perhaps more than a good many, just how important light and colour is in the conception of a railway landscape of this kind.

The 'Black 5s' were used on both passenger and freight traffic and were possessed more of a workaday image perhaps than a romantic one. A common sight in the steam era due to the large number of these engines built by the LMS. This scene shows one of the class clattering through Newcastle Junction near Stoke-on-Trent.

The Art of the Matter

An Ebb and flow of Memory and Experience

The ebb and flow of memory and experience – it's a turn of phrase I have borrowed from Edward Seago and his book *Tideline* of 1948. Seago was one of England's best landscape painters of the twentieth century, not that he ever painted railways as such – rivers and boats were more his cup of tea as the title of his book might suggest.

But I like the idea of memories ebbing and flowing, coming gently into mind, perhaps momentarily evoking pleasure through some past event or time in our lives, or maybe through someone known. That is what the paintings and this book are about.

In putting together this collection of paintings and writing about them it has inevitably involved a deal of looking back, both to my own past and the past years depicted in the subjects that have inspired the paintings. A certain time or place remembered, and of course the people who have come into my life who have significantly affected not only the work I have produced but the course my life has taken as a result.

I do not intend these various essays to become too autobiographical, but in certain circumstances it would be remiss of me to separate the painting from the story involved with it, and in what is now some forty years as a professional painter, and sixty years since I first put a brush to paper with some serious intent to become an artist, there will no doubt be a story or two here and there to recount.

My paintings bring together two very different worlds: the railway scene of the past and the present day world of traditional painting. What unites these two very different spheres of railways and art within the context of these pages is my love for them both, the one inspiring the other.

My modes of expression are therefore straightforward and I hope honest and unlike some aspects of the art world of the twenty-first century, easy to understand and painted from the heart.

Opposite page:
Elidir at Llanberis,
oil painting, size 14"x 18"

To use the term 'a passion to paint' is not too strong, for after a lifetime of doing just that I cannot possibly imagine life without being able to paint. The journey to become a professional was long and arduous but the twenty years that it took stood me in good stead despite the lack of encouragement on the part of fellow artists that I knew, all of them commercial artists by day, and fine artists in their spare time, who were convinced that a living could not be made from it.

I am glad to say they were wrong but will willingly agree that I have been extremely fortunate to have just occasionally been in the right place at the right time and to have met the right people to take forward my obsession and make that dream come true.

The first of those was perhaps an unlikely fellow in that he was a bluff Northerner who was not known for his patience, swore a bit, smoked far too much and liked his drink equally. But he had a great appreciation of oil paintings and incidentally happened to be the Curator of Historical Relics at the British Transport Museum in London. So, late in 1968, I secured an interview with him to look at my paintings – I didn't know where that might lead, by then I was clutching at straws having been turned out of gallery after gallery to get absolutely nowhere.

John Scholes was something of an enigma. He came to his position at the British Transport Museum with no background of railway matters, having been the Curator of the Castle Museum in York – something of which he was immensely proud. He was outspoken, sometimes to the point of rudeness as I found out the very first time I spoke to him on the telephone having requested the opportunity to show him my pictures. "Oh its no use you coming here. I only show famous artists here in my gallery – Terence Cuneo, Norman Wilkinson, David Shepherd and the like. They're a draw to the public do you understand, they bring people in through my doors. With all due respects to you old son, nobody's ever heard of you."

It was only my exasperated reply that if they were all like him and wouldn't even look at my blessed pictures, then nobody ever would hear of me, that eventually got me through his front door. And the rest as they say is history. My exhibition in his gallery in 1969 was the greatest turning point in my life. "I shall promote you as my discovery lad, you will become famous." For John Scholes my 'promotion' was a risk. But he prided himself that he had a good eye for a picture and indeed had added considerably to the museum's collection of paintings over the years with great success. I became very fond of him and needless to say, grateful for the chance he gave me to showcase my work and become successful. Indeed, that exhibition virtually sold out and with it an order book of commissions for well over a year – enough at least to take the plunge at last and paint full-time.

John went on after that to promote other 'unknowns' quite successfully, his eye for a good painting holding him in good stead. His work as Curator for Historical Relics was supported by a panel of knowledgeable people in the railway field and at a crucial time for the preservation of important locomotives. Many now saved from demolition and on show at Swindon, York and other locations owe their existence to the work done by John Scholes during his tenure at the British Transport Museum throughout the 1960s.

With the prospect of York becoming the venue for the proposed National Railway Museum in the early 1970s I recall John becoming very nervous about his future. The closure of his museum was a sad time for him, he had guided its success from its opening in 1961 and so it had been very much his baby. He doubted if he was up to the job of heading the new National in York if, that is, he was ever in the running for it, but certainly he thought he was. In the event, that highly prized position went to the late John Coily who was eminently suited to the post.

John Scholes died with little acclaim for what he had achieved and in a sad financial state, leaving insufficient funds for his own funeral. I remember there was a modest event at the National Railway Museum in his honour sometime afterwards championed by his friend Peter Manisty. I was asked to speak on that occasion about the man's vision in helping young artists along the way. It was a honour I was only too pleased to fulfil, being the first of John's 'discoveries'.

All that seems a long time ago now, forty years in fact have passed since that eventful day when I walked through the doors of his museum and gallery. In turn he opened for me a door to a very different future from the years preceding. A future that has proved to be a most privileged way of life – to paint as a means of earning a living and to find the most incredible support for what I do from the purchasers and collectors that have come my way over the years.

The Patron and the Artist

I would need a heck of an excuse in writing a book about my railway pictures without mentioning the name Bill McAlpine, or Sir William McAlpine BT as he should properly be addressed. Bill came into my life as a result of the exhibition at the British Transport Museum to which he had been invited by John Scholes, due also to a bit of prompting by the artist Terence Cuneo. Terence had been in to see the exhibition and wrote me a letter afterwards enthusing about the paintings. It was of course at that time a great boost to my confidence and the start of a friendship with the artist that I valued greatly.

Bill and I were of a similar age and we shared a similar passion for steam locomotives. Other than that we had little in common, coming from greatly contrasting backgrounds, but he liked my paintings and a friendship developed. His patronage during those early years of my professional career was invaluable. Not only did he buy many paintings for his home and company, but he introduced me to others who bought as a result. It was the sort of support that most raw professionals would give their right arm for.

I well remember the first time I was invited to spend a weekend at his estate near Henley. It was late in 1969 and of course I had not graduated beyond a rusty bike by then, so it necessitated a rail journey to get there. I was met at the station by his chauffeur, which heralded an introduction into a whole new world for me. To say I was somewhat green would be to put it rather mildly, so it was the start of a steep learning curve that I had to get to grips with pretty quickly.

Suddenly there I was faced with learning the procedures and etiquette of life on a country estate, and one with a private railway to boot. Oh, and of course a butler to serve at dinner! It was a very different world to my own but despite my inadequacies at the time the friendship continued apace well into the 1970s with commissions from his construction company for a variety of subjects, including the building of power stations along the Clyde, North Sea oil rigs, and many architectural subjects both in London and Scotland.

With much work in hand from other sources as well, the early years of my professional career in the seventies were exciting and rewarding, but would it continue? Those previous years of being pretty hard-up had become ingrained and it was difficult to throw off that sense of insecurity. I think it was partly this, and also the fact that I wanted to do something different in terms of railway art, that gave birth to the idea of a whole series of paintings that would look at many differing aspects of our railway's history.

My plan to paint about twenty-four large canvases (most were fifty inches by sixty inches long) would take, I estimated, about four years to complete, whilst fitting other commissions and paintings for exhibitions in between. It was an exciting proposition. I wanted to include not only the engines, from the beginning of it all with Trevithick's first locomotive to run on rails, but portraits of the designers and engineers who built them. The pre-grouping companies with their liveries and heraldry would also be a feature, and of course architectural settings with each canvas reflecting the decor of the period that it represented.

Of course, I couldn't do any of this without someone to pay for it. I talked to John Scholes about the project and after various suggestions of possible buyers he arrived at the conclusion that Bill McAlpine should be approached with the idea. I had shied away from doing that because he had already been extremely generous in his support for what I did, and I did not want to feel I was taking advantage of his generosity. John, however, saw it differently, saying that Bill could be offended if he was not offered the chance at least to consider it. So a meeting was arranged in due course and over lunch at the Dorchester we discussed the project fully with Bill, and the outcome was to my great delight a resounding 'yes' to the whole thing.

Artistically it meant a great deal. I could spread my wings and explore on these canvases a whole range of ideas that would trace the progress of locomotive design and the British railway scene in a way that had not been done before. It was very inspiring. Financially, with the payments for it spread over a four year period, I had gained a measure of the security I had hoped for, with each year's fees enabling me to assess just how much other work I accepted as a result.

It was a great position to be in so early on in my career and the following three-and-a-half years saw the collection of paintings grow into what I had always thought of as 'A History of the British Steam Locomotive', but which ultimately became known as 'The Weston Collection', a title I think decided on between Bill and the publishers of the soft-cover book that followed its display at The Royal Exchange in 1977.

The collection occupied some 135ft of wall-space and went on to tour museums and galleries throughout the UK over the next three years thanks to Bill McAlpine's generosity and his company's involvement in arranging it all.

By the end of the seventies the tour of galleries and museums was drawing to a close with an eight months' showing at the National Railway Museum in York. A decade had passed since my show at the British Transport Museum and I felt I had become in that time reasonably established, with some assurance for the future. My greatest regret was that my 'discoverer', John Scholes, had not lived long enough to witness his protégé's progress. He died in 1974, well before 'The Weston Collection' was completed and launched.

For Bill McAlpine that same decade had seen his name become synonymous with the world of railway preservation, amongst his most notable achievements was the saving of the famous locomotive 'Flying Scotsman' after its disastrous tour of America. But for his timely action in rescuing it from receivership it may never have been returned to our shores, with the consequent pleasure it has since given to hundreds of thousands of enthusiasts and the general public alike.

There have been many wealthy personalities involved in the railway preservation movement over the years and heaven knows it has been disappointing and even disastrous for some, but Bill McAlpine's name will forever stand out uniquely in the history of steam railway preservation for his considerable knowledge and contribution in so many respects, and also not least for his generosity. I hope the four paintings reproduced here will give a flavour of what the twenty-four paintings of 'The Weston Collection' portrayed both in their style and content.

British Rail's Chairman, Sir Peter Parker, visited the Weston Collection twice during its time on show to the public, first at The Royal Exchange in London, and later during its showing at The National Railway Museum at York.

He wrote about the paintings: "The story of steam is in books, in poetry and in prose. In the museums there is the hardware, the great engines themselves, the bones of a glorious past. But no-one has tried to do what David Weston has done in oils. His series of paintings give us a vivid pageant of the history of steam – there is a mastery of style here and with high passion. I am proud and happy to be associated with the collection.

For more than 3 years the artist has worked on this unique chronicle on canvas. Here we have the faces of the engineers, the pioneers, the innovators – and the faces of their engines. Here we have the crests, and intricate seals of the famous companies, letters, posters and blueprints. Here we have the reality of work on the rails, the noise of the engine sheds, the weight of the heavy iron, the stench of hot grease. Here the rise, the days of great triumph; and the fall, the graveyard stillness of the scrap heap, the solitude and the pathos of the worn-out giants at their end.

I commend this unique set of pictures for their documentary accuracy, their humanity, their grandeur, their dignity. From now on, whenever the story of the great age of steam is told, the David Weston Collection will be remembered, for it will have become part of the story."

Opposite
Four Paintings from the Weston Collection

No 1. **The Dawn of a New Era** size 50" x 60"
Richard Trevithick and the Pen-y-Darren Locomotive

No 13. **'The Great Central and the Great War'** size 50" x 60"
The Robinson 2-8-0 of 1911 and the Great Central Atlantic

No 19. **Staniers Giants of the '30s** size 50" x 60"
The Black 5 of 1934 and the Coronation Pacific of 1937

No 23. **A Carcase at Kettering** size 50" x 60"
The End of Steam

No 1

No 13

No 19

No 23

Lord Burleigh of Balfour and myself at Edinburgh

The Weston Collection at the National Railway Museum in York

Steam and Smoke at Stockport
oil painting, size 24"x 20"

Stockport in the 1960s expressed here through the inevitable steam and smoke that dominated the scene. The artist L.S. Lowry had stood here to draw sometime before I did, but what a subject! My painting depicts the atmosphere of a wet day but with plenty of light to reflect on the roofs and pavements where a few bedraggled folk hurry their way homewards.

The Class 8 ex-LMS engine and wagons were a common sight on this viaduct and for me complete what I feel is an exciting subject that says much about this part of England in the steam era.

The picture was painted on a rough canvas primed with a reddish brown base which helps the overall warmth to come through, and here and there has been allowed to show as a part of the paint texture, especially in the sky.

The Shed at Aberdare, oil painting, size 18"x 24"

This is a painting where the atmosphere of smoke and steam is just as important to the scene as are the engines themselves. Grimy, work worn engines reflect in the puddles on the ground, with rails caching the light of a brighter sky after rain.

The scene was a commissioned painting set in about 1952 and called for innumerable changes in the subtlety of the greys in the picture – warm to cool from mauves to blues and brown-greys. Just the sort of atmosphere I love to paint.

Over the Forth, oil painting, size 30"x 40"

The magnificent structure of the bridge spanning the River Forth dominates this composition and dwarfs the houses below in no uncertain terms. The drama is heightened further by the presence of the train emerging from the massive form of those central spans, with what more appropriate an engine than the 'Flying Scotsman' itself as a focal point.

The painting was done in 1974 and purchased by Bill McAlpine who hung it in his office for a while before taking it home to his museum.

The Duchess of Hamilton Under Resoration,

oil painting, size 24"x 36"

The setting for this painting is in the workshops of the National Railway Museum at York. I had been invited by the Friends of the Museum to produce a painting of this great locomotive undergoing the final stages of its return to running order.

A limited edition fine art print was produced to help the funds and the original drawing done on 14 April 1989 is reproduced here with the painting.

The boiler was at that stage held inches above its normal seating due to final work on securing the ash pan to the firebox foundation ring. If anything, this added to the impressive perspective of the composition, and when later in the day 'Green Arrow' was brought into the shed the contrast between its polished form and the matt colour of the 'Duchess' only served to heighten the conception and drama of a great locomotive under restoration.

Happily the engine's cab was strategically placed for my viewpoint to lead the eye through and beyond into the depths of the workshop, completing the scene as the museum's team went about the ongoing tasks of restoration.

One final memory of the day; I had gone prepared to work dressed in an old sweater and jeans, as normal on such an occasion. However, during the day the Museum's director, John Coily, came along to watch progress and asked if I would care to join him for a spot of lunch. Thinking this might just involve a sandwich in a local pub I agreed. What he had not told me was that the venue was to be his rotary club luncheon! Suffice it to say that I think I was the only chap there in an old sweater and jeans!

ITV promotional poster.

Cameraman Paddy Seale and Producer John Oxley on location with me at Loughborough for 'Beware of Trains'.

Outside the Shed, watercolour, size 12"x 17.5"

A loose watercolour done at Loughborough in 2004, and one that I very much enjoyed doing. I loved the general clutter of the scene with that red flag contrasting so well with the blue of the oil drum. The B1 class engine was perfectly positioned, with the light creating lovely patterns along the tender and framed by the bridge.

It is a painting that reminds me of the hours I spent in 1984 with the ATV film crew making the documentary film 'Beware of Trains'. Several sequences were shot on the Great Central's lines at Loughborough and another B1 locomotive that was there at the time was allotted to our use. It was the beautifully restored 'Mayflower' in its LNER green livery.

It was great fun as always to ride on the footplate whilst recording a sequence about the power and glamour of the steam locomotive. I remember also a rather dicey moment when cameraman Peter Sakeld nearly came to grief whilst filming on the engine.

John Oxley, the film's producer had asked Peter to get a shot of me leaning out of the cab window as we moved off down the line. In order to do this Peter had climbed on to the running-plate, operating his camera with one hand and hanging on to the handrail on the boiler with his other. But as the locomotive moved forward under the bridge a sudden and violent escape of steam from the safety valves completely enveloped the engine and terrified Peter who fell on to his back with his camera dangling close to Mayflower's driving wheels. It was a salutary experience for all concerned and a lesson learnt on the power and danger of a live steam locomotive. Peter was excused duties for the rest of the day whilst filming continued with second cameraman Paddy Seale.

It was a great experience for me over the three weeks it took to make 'Beware of Trains', and a great boost to my career on its eventual showing in 1985.

Inside the Shed, watercolour, size 12"x 18"

Another lovely subject at Loughborough. I spent a very pleasurable morning drawing the sketch for this picture which required much concentrated work to record the details of the locomotive and also more importantly how the light struck the newly-painted finish The two workmen lead the eye past the barrier of the door to the scene outside, linking the two together.

To do such a complicated subject in watercolour is not easy. One has to work around the lighter areas and highlights, putting in the darks first. In oils, although one may also paint the darker areas first, it is a relatively easy task to paint any lights on top. Not so with watercolour – it is the most demanding and difficult of all media because one has to get it about right first time. There is little room for mistakes.

Latent Power, watercolour size 13"x 19"

The combination here of two powerful images in the yards at Crewe, those of the engine and the coaling plant, make a dramatic and atmospheric painting where watercolour has been used to its maximum strength to portray the sheer size and weight of the locomotive.

Deltic Drama, oil painting, size 18"x 24"

I cannot say that diesel or electric locomotives inspire the same compulsion to paint as steam but under certain conditions of either light or location I have occasionally felt the urge to have a go.

In this picture, of what I consider to be the most impressive of diesel designs, the English Electric Deltic, I feel those elements of light and atmosphere have come together to make the locomotive come alive. It is rather more difficult, without the aid of steam and smoke, to make what is basically a box look powerful!

City of Leicester at Crewe, oil painting, size 20"x 24"

The immense power that is inherent in the design of Sir William Stanier's massive Pacific class engines was the inspiration for this study of black engines on a dark day of intermittent rain. Reflections on the wet walkways between the foreground tracks and glistening on the locomotives, create a complexity of close tones and colours that, within the black livery, shone from mauves and blues to lilacs and rusts.

Being a Leicester lad I felt I just had to paint this particular locomotive. The setting of the busy yards at Crewe create, together with the steam and smoke, the perfect background for the enormous bulk of the engine and the feeling of latent power that this portrait of 46252 expresses.

Snow on the Southern, watercolour, size 13"x 20"

There was always a thrill in watching trains in the snow For me, as a painter, the transformation of the landscape gave an added incentive to take out a sketchbook to record the railway scene in its almost monochromatic appearance under a blanket of white snow.

This picture, painted in watercolour, is set somewhere on the line between Guildford and Reading. The ubiquitous Maunsell Mogul, working hard at the head of its train of Southern green coaches, contrasts with the warm shades of the bridge and the cool blues and greys of the snow-covered landscape.

Freight on the Central Line, watercolour, size 11.5"x 18"

The sight of a locomotive working hard throwing a huge plume of smoke skywards always made a stirring sight. Here on the Great Central north of Leicester I so often watched these ROD locomotives hauling their endless train of wagons.

This is a free-style watercolour done pretty well throughout on first wet and then damp watercolour paper. The sky and smoke were painted on very wet paper but with much care to control the washes. Then, as the paper began to dry out, the landscape and lineside features were dropped in. The engine and track came together last of all as the paper dried and allowed the harder lines of the locomotive to be painted without the watercolour running too much.

Castle on the Coast, oil painting, size 20"x 30"

One can hardly look at this well-known spot without thinking of holidays and long summer days by the sea. Warm sunshine and glorious copper-capped engines every so often gave us the ingredients of a holiday that would be hard to beat if the lure of steam was within one's blood. This painting of Castle class locomotive 'Tintagel Castle' rounding the bend at Teignmouth reflects those thoughts, especially when one realises that just at the left, below the railings, is the sea and shore itself.

Quorn and Woodhouse Box,
watercolour, size 13"x 10"

Coming out of Leicester, oil painting, size 12"x 16"

Forest Road Box forms the main feature of this composition where a grimy B1 locomotive passes by on its way from Leicester's Belgrave Road Station to the seaside at Skegness.

The bridge that the train is emerging from carries the Midland main line, so Forest Road was always a great spot to watch trains go by. But for me the attractive architecture of the little signal box was enough to make me open the sketchpad on more than one occasion.

Oakdale Colliery, watercolour, size 12"x 17"

The drama of the South Wales collieries is epitomized in this composition where the conglomeration of buildings, culminating in the pit-head winding gear, come together to make an irresistible subject for a line and wash watercolour. For the eagle-eyed there is a locomotive in there somewhere, busying itself amongst the grime and smoke. Oakdale resulted in about four or five paintings in both oil and watercolour over the years – the brief sketches I did there standing me in good stead. But I wish I had done more.

Mallard at Grantham, oil painting, size 20"x 30"

The A4 Pacific locomotive No 22 'Mallard' passes Grantham South signal box in its splendid garter blue livery and hauling its train of Pullman coaches. I set this period piece on a day of sunshine and showers which gave me the best opportunity to have reflections and reflected lights on the ground and tracks.

'Mallard' was repainted in garter blue in 1948 and given the usual stainless steel numbers on its cab sides although the tender was painted British Railways following the recent takeover from the LNER.

I remember at about that time standing on Grantham station as the A4 'William Whitelaw' drew in, having recently been outshopped in the blue livery. What a splendid sight! I had a job to stop my hands from shaking with excitement as I tried to photograph her with my Box Brownie camera. It came out alright as I remember, well the best a Box Brownie could manage, but the photo has long since disappeared into the ether like so many others I took at the time. How I wish I had them now.

Steam at Stamford, watercolour, size 12"x 17"

The handsome architecture of the station at Stamford in Lincolnshire is the focal point for this painting. Built of the local limestone it still remains in use although unfortunately it is more likely to be a rather boring DMU that pulls in than a lively steam locomotive.

Kettle and Cans, oil painting 7.25"x 6.75"

The Master Cutler, oil painting, size 16"x 20"

The engine is the famous 'Flying Scotsman' departing Leicester on The Master Cutler, Sheffield to Marylebone express. 'Flying Scotsman' was for a time shedded at Leicester during the latter years of the steam age so its appearance in my part of the world for a while was commonplace.

This picture was commissioned by Don Kendall whose father George had often driven the engine and the inset to bottom left of the painting depicts him looking out from the footplate at Aylesbury station, cup of tea in hand!

City of London, oil painting, size 24"x 36"

Stanier's magnificent locomotive 'City of London' on shed at Crewe.

Deltic at York, oil painting, size 24"x 36"

King Haakon, oil painting, size 24"x 36"

Rothley station on the old Great Central Line, south of Loughborough is the setting for this painting. The Norwegian locomotive was owned during its stay on the Great Central's preserved lines by the late Tony Parker. Tony was one of the nicest men I have ever known in the steam preservation field and when he commissioned this painting from me in 1977 I set about it with great pleasure.

'Haakon', as Tony called her, is not a beautiful engine, nor is she particularly majestic. But certainly there is an enormous character in her makeup and a unique balance of shapes and fittings that imbue the engine with an immense aesthetic appeal, which to me as an artist was irresistible.

Incidentally, when 'King Haakon' first came to this country, after surviving the rigours of the war years in Norway, I was asked by its then owner, Gerald Pegano, to design the nameplates that the locomotive now bears. That was a pleasure and no problem whatsoever – the problem really lay in where on earth any nameplate could be sited on a locomotive already smothered in hardware!

I am indebted to Tony's wife Pat, a good friend of ours, for her permission to reproduce the painting here.

A Return to Rothley

There is a stretch of line between Leicester and Loughborough on the old Great Central route where the three intervening stations were built in the style adopted by that railway, displaying their stylish architecture in the local red brick with spacious entrance stairways.

Of the first, just on the outskirts of the city, nothing remains today thanks to the vandals who saw it off well before those responsible for the restoration of the line could save it. But nonetheless two other similar do remain handsomely restored to their former glories. Quorn and Woodhouse in the LNER style and colour, and Rothley taken back to how it was in the Great Central's years.

The latter is my favourite. Its gas lamps glow in the evening twilight, all is kept smart on the platforms bedecked with flowers, and the baggage and ticket offices evoke the atmosphere of those days long gone, in abundance.

Vintage enamel signs at Rothley Station.

It is good now to sit here quietly from time to time just to reflect on my younger years. Those long hot summer days. They were long and hot weren't they? Lying in the grass beside the lines, waiting to hear the hiss of the signal wires, and then the anticipation as the distant beat of a locomotive heralded its imminent arrival at the station. Sometimes the anticipation was better than the event but at other times a 'Director' or 'Sandringham' class engine may well have sidled in with a local from Nottingham or maybe Sheffield.

A few minutes of chatter, clatter and shouts, a shrill whistle whilst carriage doors slammed and a toot from the engine before it effortlessly slipped away into the distant landscape. Calm was once more restored to this little oasis now deserted

Careful restoration at Rothley.

again and one was left to enjoy the unique nature of the architecture – it intrigued me even then as a boy – and perhaps what was so much a part of every railway station, those lovely old enamel advertising signs.

They bring so much back to us now of the way we were – advising us what to eat and drink, how to clean our homes, what petrol we should use in our car (if we had one in those days), and oh dear, what cigarettes we should be smoking. They belong to an age that showed itself in so many respects up to the mid 1950s when the new upbeat Britain began to unnecessarily get rid of so much from our past.

Remembering the trains of the middle years of the last century is made easy at Rothley by its careful restoration and attention to the smallest detail. An obliging booking clerk would issue a ticket from the rack above his desk and a porter would be on hand to help one aboard with the luggage. Oh yes, and of course there would have been a guards' van – what a good idea! – in case one was taking a bicycle or something equally cumbersome on the journey.

One might pity the poor chap with a bike today, as I witnessed recently on board a local DMU, struggling along an overcrowded centre aisle pushing his bike ahead of him in search of somewhere, anywhere, for pity's sake, to safely stow it. He ended with it standing upright next to the doors! What might have happened in the event of an emergency stop does not bear thinking about. Health and Safety? Oops.

It was an uncomfortable journey made more so by a girl opposite telling all and sundry on her mobile phone about the underwear she had bought in 'Bras 'R Us'! Travelling on that train with people constantly talking loudly on mobile phones almost made me yearn for the quiet of the old single compartment trains – even if there were no loos on board!

Comfort for passengers has advanced in most respects since the days of the old single compartments with their horsehair-stuffed seats and watercolours under the luggage racks, although the loss of the lovely pictures is certainly regrettable, done as they were by some of the leading artists of the day. It is sad to observe that respect for one's fellow passengers in some instances has not always advanced to the same degree. Did we, I wonder, have more time and more respect for one another over half a century ago?

I have a brief but telling memory from my childhood following the conclusion of hostilities over the last war. My mother and father had decided that a celebratory holiday would be in order and so off we set on the train from Leicester to Morecambe. I expect it would have been at Crewe as we sat in a stationary carriage awaiting the off, when right by our window a Coronation Pacific locomotive very slowly and quietly glided by, as its nameplate by degrees revealed itself to be that of 'King George VI'. The whole compartment quite involuntarily stood up! And then, rather embarrassed, sat down again in their seats. Such was the respect for King and Country in those days – a nation proud to be British.

I have an O gauge model in the studio of that engine in its British Railways red livery. It reminds me each time I look at it of that fleeting memory and my question "Why did they stand up Daddy?" "It's the King lad, the King". A small incident, but it impressed itself on my memory as a ten-year-old in the 1940s. Of course, such behaviour would be considered quite ludicrous today, and indeed it was of its time, but in the mobile-mad world of the twenty-first century it seems a shame not to be able to relish train travel in the same way that I used to do.

Thinking of my model of the 'King', locomotive liveries are another thing that change has not always favoured for the better. Sometimes now I find myself cringing when a train pulls into the station, looking like something more suited to a fairground with its computer-designed livery. It is supposed by those who condone and accept it to be modern and forward-thinking. Whatever happened to good design and restrained colour? That in my book spoke far more for a company's image than the razzmatazz of the present day, especially so where our transport systems are concerned.

At least one would be spared such sights arriving alongside the platform at Rothley. Like all those other Rothleys up and down the country on preserved lines they are in a wider sense a small reflection of English life in the middle part of the twentieth century. England in the 1950s saw a country in transi-

tion, the vagaries of a World War still lingered but the face of the country seen in the streets of our towns and cities was increasingly one of colour and immense individuality. Of course, it was far from perfect; our homes for the majority were drab and our health lacked the benefits of today's advanced technology. But there was a distinct air of optimism and a pronounced sense of communities pulling together following the war years that bred a healthy respect for one another, and much of that has regrettably become lost over the years since.

That individuality I write of regarding England's past showed itself in numerous ways. Every shop in every village and town was different – an expression of the owner's personality and quirks One saw it also in our transport systems where their differing liveries added more colour to the streets and city corporations ran tramcars and buses proudly displaying their individual liveries and crests. It all made one city very different to another, unlike today's excessive uniformity.

Within the streets, architecture that had survived the war years and stood for decades made each city, town and village unique. So much of that was quite indiscriminately destroyed as the 50s drew to a close. We saw great country houses demolished in the countryside, and the village shop together with many other small concerns become ousted by large chain stores, whilst planners and developers who seem unable to this day to have any understanding for the history and the integrity of England's individual regions accepted brashness and mediocrity in much of what replaced the old and what was by them considered to be outdated.

The railways of course were very much part of it all. They had served their four separate regions for decades, adding considerably to the diversity of the country's character and charm throughout those years. The zenith of the 'big four's' steam years came in the 1930s with the development of high speed and streamlined locomotives that remained unsurpassed for the next twenty years.

Paramount amongst my own memories of those magnificent machines of the 1930s, where design was just as important to their creators as was performance and engineering excellence, were Sir Nigel Gresley's streamlined locomotives that I constantly saw at Grantham and were a spectacular example of brilliant design that echoed much from the art deco years, and that for me really said it all.

Their contrast, with their equally splendid counterparts on the LMS of the period and the Southern Railways Merchant Navy Pacifics, simply underlined the enormous variety of design amongst main line motive power that those of us lucky enough to have enjoyed the years of the 1950s and earlier can look back on with much pleasure. But of course it wasn't just the locomotives and rolling stock where the railways handed down a rich heritage. The pre-grouping company's care in building stations and lineside structures that reflected the architectural style of the area, and blended so well into the British countryside, was in many cases exemplary.

Unfortunately so many of these architectural gems bit the dust in lessons never learned but now regretted as the obsessive desires of the late 50s and 1960s to standardise everything, from our towns and cities themselves, to the merest detail within them, took a hold with a vengeance.

I have no doubt that my ticket to Rothley is tinged to a slight degree by the rosy glow of nostalgia for an English way of life that has passed into history, but when I see a constant string of juggernauts clogging up the streets of my local market town I cannot help but think back despairingly to those days prior to 1964 when the new Chairman of British Railways, Dr Richard Beeching, began his destruction of so many far-reaching branchlines, closing a third of Britain's rail networks into the bargain and, on those that were spared, over another 2000 stations suffered closure.

With the loss of such an enormous number of rail links to our towns and villages it was inevitable that whole communities would change. The railway station had within living memory been a focal point in town and country alike – a place of greetings and of farewells. The England that my generation grew up into, despite the lingering effects of the war years, was still one with a unique identity – we took it for granted I'm afraid, expecting it always to be the same.

I am not for one moment laying the blame for the demise of all I have touched on to the decisions for the elimination of the country's branchlines or even on the railways in general. But the immensity of what happened under the Beeching axe certainly did nothing to protect what we had gone through two World Wars to preserve, and only exacerbated that rate of change that the 1960s heralded with open arms.

Keeping the aspidistra watered.

It may be difficult for those who never knew the 40s and 50s to fully understand just what it is that we have lost in the character of England having never known it, or of a way of life that certainly reflected a less avaricious society and a much less pressured time than today's speeded up existence allows.

Rothley station and all those other places like it on our preserved railways can only hint at what it was like in those years, but for some it is a starting point for that ebb and flow of memory as it has been for me – some happy, others that have led to the odd rant! But it is nice on visiting these little oases of calm to let the imagination wander in the pretence at least that time has maybe stood still.

So here's to all those who keep those enamel signs twinkling in the sunlight, lovingly tend their white edged flower-beds, and water the aspidistra on the waiting room table. Without them these little pockets of England's past would be gone forever.

Rothley Station
Great Central Railway,
11 August 2003.

Rothley, watercolour, size 20"x 19"

Nothing of the prettiness of the country station in this painting. It is of a Rothley seen well after the last train of the day had departed, a lonely platform and a dramatic late-evening image using watercolour at its full strength.

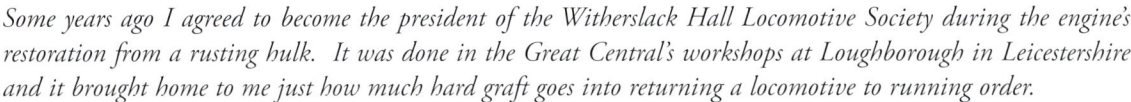

Witherslack Hall, oil painting, size 20"x 30"

Some years ago I agreed to become the president of the Witherslack Hall Locomotive Society during the engine's restoration from a rusting hulk. It was done in the Great Central's workshops at Loughborough in Leicestershire and it brought home to me just how much hard graft goes into returning a locomotive to running order.

Eventually all those involved watched with pride as the engine was put into steam again and I did my bit in unveiling the nameplate before a good crowd of spectators at Loughborough station.

The Great Western Hall class were a development of the earlier Saint class and each engine was named after a country estate – Witherslack Hall being in Lancashire. My painting depicts the locomotive at rest in Old Oak Common shed on a day of fleeting sunlight and shadow.

Unvieling the nameplate of 'Witherslack Hall'.

Photographer Colin Garratt and myself compare notes with work for the Jessop Collection.

Witherslack Hall on Freight, oil painting, size 14"x 18"

The engine at work and at speed on a mixed freight, painted as a part of the 'Jessop Collection', a touring exhibition of paintings and photographs in conjunction with Colin Garratt the photographer, and sponsored by the photographic chain, Jessops. Alan Jessop had become a collector of my paintings and the idea of a collaboration between an artist and a photographer sprang out of discussions with him which his company ultimately promoted.

The collection was shown at many venues including the National Railway Museum in York, and consisted of forty of my smaller oils, nothing larger than 16" x 20" and an equal number of Colin's photographs framed to a similar size. Many of Colin's photographs depict the colour and atmosphere of the railway scene and in many ways compliment my own way of looking at the subject. The exhibition ran for about three years and was a most rewarding experience for both Colin and myself.

Opposite
William Mason, oil painting, size 20"x 30"

As Vice President of the Ortner Freight Car Company in Cincinnati, Ohio, Henry Keniston travelled the world each year. It was on a visit to England that he glimpsed through the windows of the City Art Gallery in Portsmouth the paintings of the Weston Collection. It was enough to draw him in to view the exhibition with the result that he commissioned me to do a portrait of his Company President, Joe Ortner, together with some of the wagons that they produced.

The outcome brought many unexpected pleasures, amongst which was an invitation for Mary and I to visit Cincinnati to unveil the portrait and spend some time with Henry and his wife Jane. It was the start of a lovely friend-ship which this painting vividly brings to mind for me. On a glorious hot summer's day during 1980 the four of us visited the roundhouse of the Baltimore and Ohio railroad in Baltimore, a short car ride from Washington DC where we had been staying.

Henry's enthusiasm for railroads was infectious and I have many happy memories of the various commissions he favoured me with, both personally and for his company. Unfortunately, nothing ever remains the same forever and Henry died some time before I had painted this canvas of 'William Mason' for him. The Ortner Freight Car Company asked me to complete the commission and as I progressed the picture my thoughts returned again to that day when we stood before this great veteran of the Baltimore and Ohio Railroad. Henry told me something of its history and the part that these old wood-burners played in the turmoil of America's Civil War.

In a corner of the shed at Baltimore stood an old horse-drawn Connestoga Wagon and it was Henry's wish that this reminder of America's past should be included in the painting.

The late Henry Keniston.

A Portrait of Alan Bloom

1907–2005

There is a sorry tale to tell about this painting (opposite). I completed it in 1971 and wanted to portray not only the man as I knew him, but some of the notable engines that at that time had recently formed a part of his new steam museum at Bressingham in Norfolk.

The picture was exhibited with Alan's blessing in a one-man show I had been invited to stage in the engineering block at Leicester University during that same year. Unfortunately someone took exception to this particular painting and slashed it right across Alan's face, ripping the canvas to such an extent that the painting had to be withdrawn from the show. Quite why this should happen and in such a location I shall never know for the perpetrator was never caught. It upset Alan considerably and although the damage could be repaired he asked me to do a second painting identical to the first, which under the circumstances I happily agreed to do for him.

The second version is now held with a collection of my paintings by the museum and family at Bressingham. Ordinarily I would never do an identical copy of a subject. One may well use a subject more than once but then it would be presented in a totally different way, different colour, lighting, or a shift in the composition etc. To do a second one of Alan was however no hardship – this first one was taken in by the insurers and I was paid for its full value. Seeing the second version hanging in the sitting room at Bressingham Hall was a constant reminder on my visits there of what had happened so I was never able to completely forget about the incident. Then in 2006, some thirty-five years later, I received a telephone call from Susan Canderton whom it transpired had inherited the first painting from Philip Holt, her uncle. He had purchased it from the insurers for whom he worked at the time, at a very advantageous price, in 1972, and consequently had it fully restored to its original condition.

Alan's reaction to the damage of his portrait revealed the more sensitive side to his nature. Essentially a rather private man he tried to keep his personal and home life apart from the public figure that visitors to his gardens and museum at Bressingham came to know. Not so easy when you reside in the middle of it all. The image of the man that many would recall is that of a smoke-blackened figure in overalls

Alan and myself aboard Gwynedd

and a railwayman's cap, driving either one of the two ex-Penrhyn engines on the narrow gauge line that ran around the estate, indeed very much as I painted him in 1971.

By then we had become close friends and I was privileged to witness the progress as the steam museum developed into a collection of some national importance. For me as an artist in the early years of a professional career Alan's encouragement and the facilities his museum provided was of tremendous help. I could draw and paint there to my heart's content and as the years went on enjoyed several exhibitions of my paintings there including a season's showing of the Weston Collection.

But of course Alan Bloom had made Bressingham famous for its wonderful gardens well before the steam museum became a reality. First and foremost a plantsman with many books on the subject to his name, he was recognised and celebrated well beyond our shores. The Royal Horticultural Society awarded Alan the Victoria Medal of Honour and the Veitch Memorial Medal for his work.

My memories are of a truly remarkable man whose energy even into very old age was boundless and he bore his fame as an horticulturalist of international repute with great modesty.

I expect we made an odd pairing; an artist and a gardener brought together by a passion for steam engines, but there were some similarities in the way we had each pursued our separate careers. Alan had for the most part achieved his goals and his fame from within the gates of his estate at Bressingham, and I likewise have declined the use of an agent or gallery even though those offers did come along eventually, preferring to paddle my own canoe and restrict sales of my pictures from within the confines of the Lazy Acre.

It was a tricky decision to make in 1985 when we built a gallery separate to the studio in the garden. Would just one show each year, together with commissions, yield enough income to live comfortably? The years have proved positive in that respect as word spread about the October exhibition which now draws people from all over the UK and often results in a sell-out.

It has been the sort of success I could only have dreamed about back in the early seventies when we spent so much time at Bressingham Hall. Alan and his wife Flora made Mary and I so welcome on our stays there and our daughter, Karen, became friends with their daughters Anthea and Jenny, consequently spending the whole of her summer school holidays with them.

Those early years at Bressingham were for me, and I think for many, the best. Alan's foresight in providing a safe home for engines deemed worthy of preservation by British Rail's board at a time when John Scholes and his team were hard-pushed to find safe-keeping for them was paying off handsomely in terms of visitors to the gardens and museum. It had of course been quite a gamble on Alan's part to spend a huge amount of money on the erection of the museum engine shed with absolutely no guarantee that John Scholes or British Rail would agree on their engines going to East Anglia, and to a place with no rail link to boot.

My recollection of those years of the early seventies are of the optimism that abounded there on the part of the staff, volunteers and of course the family. Flora owned the Golden Gallopers roundabout which added enormously to the atmosphere of the Thursday and Sunday openings with its Chiappa organ playing gaily. On Sundays in the garden, whilst eating an ice cream or a jam doughnut from Bumshi's mobile van, one could listen to the Diss Silver Band giving their rendition of Souza or Strauss. It was all rather ad hoc but therein lay its great charm. Word spread rapidly and the gate receipts grew, ensuring growth over the following years. But with that came the inevitable problems of managing a much larger organisation on the museum side with the eventual opening of seven days a week. It led of course to the loss of that spirited show that the twice-a-week family affair style of openings had generated in an enthusiastic public, but which those of us who were closely involved (and who enjoyed the perspective of a view from outside the gates) were concerned might happen.

Alan's vision of Bressingham Steam Museum becoming a collection of diversity and importance for international locomotives was fulfilled to a certain extent, as was his desire to see such engines as 'The

A busy Sunday at the Museum

Duchess of Sutherland' and 'The Royal Scot' reside in his museum after rescuing them from the vagaries of the sea air at Butlins holiday camps where they, together with others, had been on display as visitor attractions.

Their safekeeping at Bressingham, however, together with the Britannia Pacific 'Oliver Cromwell', in time became an irritation to many rail enthusiasts who felt such giants of the steam age should not be locked away in Norfolk when they could be restored to working order for main line specials on designated routes throughout the country. It led to some hurtful and unwarranted criticism in both the railway and national press for Alan Bloom who had been an early and significant figure in terms of the steam railway preservation movement in this country, and whose actions during those years between 1968 and the mid-seventies had saved some important locomotives from possible destruction. He was never a wealthy man in financial terms and at times had to put himself and the whole future of the Bressingham estate in jeopardy to further his plans for the museum, but he had the courage to put his money where his mouth was, which is a lot more than could be said for some of his critics in terms of their contribution to the cause.

Sketches at Bressingham.

However one views the achievements of Alan Bloom, be it through his writing or the creation of his beautiful gardens, or the building of a fine steam museum, one has to acknowledge the spirit of a man who on his own doorstep could cram so much interest into his life, and by the same token give pleasure to the thousands who came and will continue to come through his gates.

Maid Marian at Bressingham, mixed media, size 12"x 15.5"

During the early 1970s these little Welsh quarry engines occupied a line within the big shed at Bressingham. The ink drawing done there at the time shows the ex Penrhyn locomotive 'George Sholto' with that powerful foreground image of the vice and workbench. A few days later, and it was the ex-Dinorwic engine 'Maid Marian' that took a similar position and this very recent painting, completed in 2008, reflects the atmosphere within the shed on that occasion. 'Maid Marian' ran on the Nursery Line at Bressingham for a short period, and was operated by the society that restored her.

This painting is one where I have used four different media for a strong effect – black ink, watercolour, acrylics and gouache. I wanted the second engine in the picture to be a mere suggestion of its presence, seen through steam and smoke and against the light of the doorway, very vague and atmospheric.

Steam at Hamburg, oil painting, size 20"x 30"

In 1971 I made a visit with Alan to Hamburg, primarily in search of an engine similar to this one, a classic for his museum at Bressingham. We were made most welcome by the railway authorities at Hamburg and I was privileged to have the freedom of the shed there for photography and drawing.

We also got to ride on the footplate of several locomotives which was a real bonus. For me the aggressive appearance of these Teutonic giants made for dramatic imagery and, together with the setting of the turntable and shed, provided all that was necessary for a first-rate composition.

A Century of The Great Eastern,
watercolour, size 8.5"x 12"

Landscape With Carriages, watercolour, size 10"x 16"

Travellers on the road between North Walsham and Aylsham in deepest Norfolk cannot fail to have noticed two venerable Great Eastern Railway carriages at Manor Farm, Banningham.

Depicted here in this rather atmospheric scene is what remains of the pair, now in a sad condition and well beyond the capabilities of the most enthusiastic preservationist to bring them back to former glories.

The one on the left in the painting is said by experts to have been built in 1895, whilst the other, whose builder's plate may be seen in the accompanying photograph, dates from 1905. They arrived at Manor Farm during the years of the last war to be used for storage and as a workshop facility – a function they just still provide. Others came to the village at the same time from the railway, one to be used as the local post office!

They are an evocative relic of the old Great Eastern Railway and have inspired me to paint no fewer than three paintings of them so far, two of which are reproduced here.

Memories and Paintings from an Industrial Landscape

My earliest memories of watching industrial locomotives at work was at some time in the 1940s during visits to an aunt's house at Desborough in Northamptonshire. A rickety one-plank footbridge crossed the quarry near the village where ironstone was being extracted, and one could look down on the proceedings from a great height breathing in the smoke from the engines below. As a child it was fascinating to watch, if not a little scary. Known as 'shaky bridge' one could bounce up and down on the structure enough at least to make one's heart beat a little faster.

But there were more than the engines to take a boy's interest in the quarries in and around Desborough. Massive, ancient and disreputable Ruston-Bucyrus excavation plant lurched to and fro, adding considerable excitement to the scene, whilst tipping the rich ochre-coloured rock into the little waggons behind the locomotive.

As a seven- or eight-year-old I understood little of the reason for all this activity, I just found it exciting to watch. In later years of course I learnt what it was all about and returned to the area to draw what there was left before it disappeared for good.

Northamptonshire was rich in ironstone and had many such railway systems, both in standard and narrow gauges.

At Kettering was the wonderful 3ft gauge tramway system that served the furnaces of the Kettering Coal & Iron Company. Their rails ran from their quarries just south of Rothwell, next door to Desborough, through some three miles of countryside to the furnaces on the outskirts of Kettering. Furnaces always make great subjects to paint but the real joy at Kettering lay in the diminutive and utterly charming locomotives that were in daily use there. Two 0-4-0 saddle-tanks built by Black, Hawthorn & Company dated from 1879 and 1885 – two wonderful Victorian curiosities which I painted several times. They were accompanied by just three slightly larger 0-6-0 saddle tanks of a similar date, given a year or two, built by Manning Wardle & Co. I loved both types, they were great Victorian oddities, quirky to

Opposite
The Barclay at Merthyr Vale
watercolour, size 12"x 19"

extreme in their designs, and spoke of the past as only the engines in industry could do during the 1940s and indeed through to the 60s.

The fact that so many of the engines working in industry, were so old and of fascinating design, is what made me want to paint them, and of course still does. I have a particular passion for the tramways of the ironstone industry, engrained no doubt from my experiences on that shaky bridge at Desborough. I found the modes of operation on these lines amazing, from the wobbly track the trains ran along, to the characters of the men that drove the engines and worked in the quarries with very little respect in those days for health and safety in their day-to day-operations.

The two letters reproduced here from the Loddington Ironstone Company, again in Northamptonshire, clearly illustrate something of those characters and their workaday lives. I have a small collection of

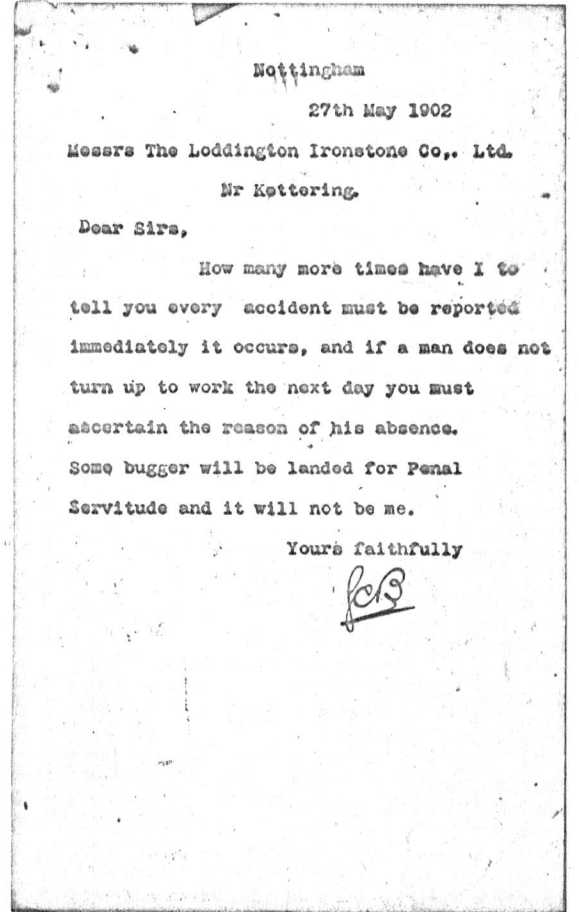

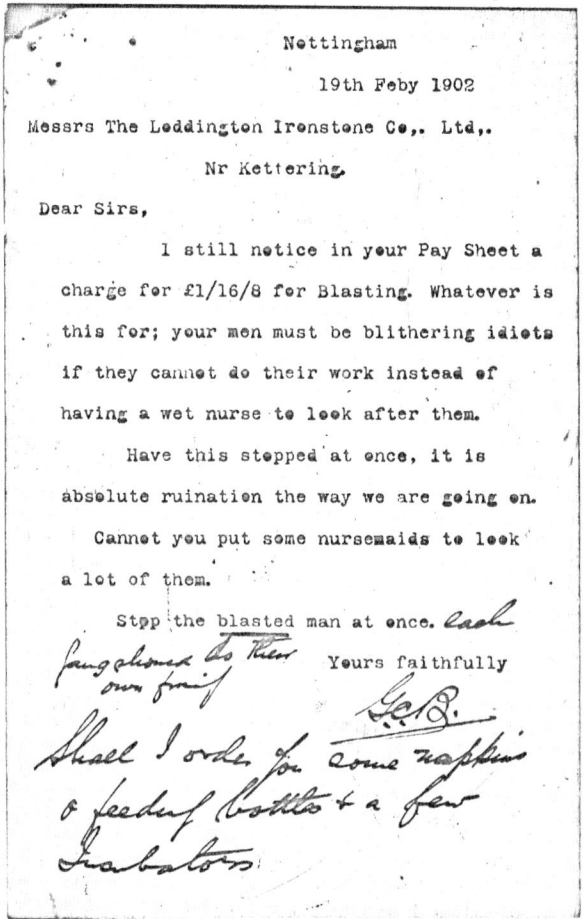

these letters, some which are so outrageous that perhaps I ought not reproduce them here! But I have selected a couple of the shorter and milder ones written by a certain GCB at Mann's Chambers in Nottingham. His forthright tone certainly makes his intentions pretty clear but heaven knows what would happen if such letters were sent out today. It seems that in 1902 it was tolerated. I just love his handwritten notes at the bottom of the letters, a final flourish in an attempt to vent his persistent anger!

Leicestershire, my home county, also had its fair share of ironstone workings, many of which ran north of Melton Mowbray into the beautiful Vale of Belvoir where rich deposits of the red-brown Marlstone were to be found, as opposed to the Northampton sand seen further south. Each quarry had its own peculiarities and stable of rumbling old locomotives. It is the memories of these operations that led me to build a model of just such a narrow gauge system, complete with its quarry and engine yard, in a part of one room of my studio. The photographs show the character of the system which I have dated at some time in the 1950s when buildings, plant and locomotives would have been in a run-down condition. I have tried to portray the atmosphere of both the quarry and the engine yard with its disused shed and rusting water tower etc. Making a model such as this is rather like painting a picture in the third dimension. I love model-making; it comes as a release from the pressures of picture making which are always ongoing. The studio houses several dioramas which model everything from a blacksmith's forge to an artist's studio.

During the years prior to my becoming a full-time painter I spent some time at the Brush Electrical Company painting in their construction shops – mostly Type 4 diesel locomotives, and also in their refurbishment shop, to gain experience of working in an industrial environment. I had an arrangement where I could go in night or day to paint and it proved to be a great learning curve.

It was shortly after that experience that I secured permission to do the same thing at the great steel works of Stewarts & Lloyds at Corby. I spent a lot of time within the steelworks and also at Pen Green engine shed which serviced the forty miles of railway throughout their quarries.

The engines were mostly Kitsons and Manning Wardles, looking resplendent in their dark green livery, but I was very fond of old 'Rhos', No.39 built in 1918 by Hudswell Clarke, and I painted a couple of pictures of her inside the shed. I liked the shape of 'Rhos' and was also attracted to the engine being the only one of the entire fleet at Pen Green to have outside cylinders. It was good to watch these sturdy engines at work in the quarries where they were often dwarfed by the sheer size of the excavations. Oakley quarry was one of the sites I visited and it was here that I watched their massive walking dragline in operation. It was the biggest machine of its kind in the world and I did a painting of it at close quarters towering over the depths of the quarry below.

Those months I spent at Corby during 1967–68 were invaluable as a part of my education in learning about steam engines and how to express my thoughts on them through the medium of paint.

The paintings that are reproduced in the following section once again reflect my use of both oils and watercolours. Often an ink line is used with the watercolour. I feel it suits these sort of subjects particularly well and allows me to be fairly free with the watercolour washes, giving movement and therefore avoiding a more static effect. Some of these reflect the work I have done within the coal industry. Apart from the pits in Leicestershire I made many visits during the 1970s and 80s to the coalfields of South Wales which have resulted in several paintings over the years. The landscape surrounding the Welsh pits so often added much to the overall pictorial effects and composition of these paintings.

Another favourite venue for painting, particularly during the middle 1960s, was the old engine shed in the granite quarry at Mountsorrel in Leicestershire. By then a bit of a ramshackle structure it was interesting in having been built on a slight curve. Inside, the Peckett 0-4-0 saddle tank locomotive 'Elizabeth' usually murmured to herself after a day's work. On Saturday afternoons I could have the place to myself, not a soul to be seen throughout the entire works and nothing whatsoever to stop anyone from wandering in, despite the various hazards of the antiquated plant still in use.

On one such delightful Saturday afternoon I was suddenly surprised by a solitary workman who looked hard at my oil painting which was in the first stages of being massed in with its approximate shapes. "Are you trying to paint t'ode engine then?" I must admit his term 'trying to paint' rankled a little and by that time in my career I prided myself that I could at least paint a 'half-decent locomotive. But nonetheless I replied calmly, "Yes, but as you can see I am only just beginning". "Oh ah, I can see that, my nephew's trying to paint and he's no good at it either"!

Oh well, C'est la vie!

The Model Railway

Activity in the quarry (above).

The rusting water tower and 'Jason' (top right).

The engine shed – in a sad state of repair (middle right).

The engine yard. A tram engine arrives with the workmen's coach for the day (bottom right).

Steam at Snibston, oil painting, size 10"x 14"

It was in 2001 that I had a retrospective exhibition of my industrial and railway paintings on show at the Snibston Discovery Park in Leicestershire.

Snibston was the site of one of the county's large number of collieries and now forms a part of a splendid industrial museum. On the opening day a special steam-up was organised and this little engine (NCB No.4 area) was one of the attractions. The painting is a recent one done from some photographs taken on the day.

At the opening of my retrospective exhibition at Snibston Discovery Park, Leicestershire in 2001.

Coal, Smoke and Steam Power, watercolour, size 13"x 19"

A thoroughly wet day in the Welsh coalfields, the tank engine reflecting light along its top and standing out in relief against the enclosing background of the pit.

Hafodyrynys Colliery was set in a deep wooded valley, unlike any other colliery I visited and drew in South Wales. The architecture of the pit was not particularly appealing but seen drenched in the atmosphere that my painting portrays it made a dramatic statement about the grim nature of the pits and life within them.

Steelworks, watercolour, size 8.5"x 19" (1968)

This painting was done at Corby in 1968 and is an example of the vigorous ink and wash technique that I did at the time. The vast complex of Stewart & Lloyds steelworks is shown here in abundance, and from my vantage point for this picture one could watch the company's engines going about their business within the works. The main line railway tracks were in the foreground although not shown in the painting.

Of course there is nothing of this left today and forty years on this painting has survived amongst the small collection of my earlier works to remind me of the wonderful subjects that abounded at Corby all those years ago.

Corby Steel, watercolour, size 12.5"x 13.75"

So many times I stood in this spot during the 1960s to watch the comings and goings of the great steel works at Corby in Northamptonshire. The yellow-painted works' engines bustled to and fro constantly and the painting expresses the activity of the day, with the complex of the steel plant making an impressive backdrop to the composition.

This picture was painted in 2004 from one of those old drawings done at the time and is owned by our friends Sue and Peter Williams who have an enormous collection of my paintings.

Light on The Grand Union, watercolour, size 13"x 18"

The old Great Central line rode high through the centre of Leicester and this watercolour, painted in 2005, is a vivid reminder of the bridges that crossed both road and canal at various points in the city centre.

This bridge covering The Grand Union Canal has long since gone but before it was demolished I did several drawings, viewing it from both sides, and have painted it since in oils above once with an engine and train on the bridge. I chose this one for the book however because the picture has that air of disuse and loneliness about it, and I liked the light with its reflection on the water. It transforms a mundane industrial scene into one of beauty.

Moonlight on the Canal, oil painting, size 12"x 16"

A view looking the other way to the one opposite. It is seen from the lovely old cast-iron Slater Street bridge which has long since disappeared. It had great character, but has since been replaced with a hideous concrete monstrosity!

Steam at the Ironworks, oil painting, size 12"x 16"

A portrait of one of my favourite industrial engines – the Manning Wardle 0-6-0 locomotive of 1869. She is seen here against a background of the furnaces at Kettering and on the bridge spanning the ore bank.

Painted in 2008 from photographs taken in the early 1960s.

Kettering Veteran, watercolour, size 9"x 12.25"

This loose watercolour was painted to express something of the detail and great character of these hard working little engines by Black, Hawthorn & Co., manufactured in 1879 and still working in 1961 when I drew her.

Cauldrons of Fire, oil painting, size 14"x 18"

The fascinating spectacle of molten waste from the furnaces being tipped on to the slag banks made a great subject from quite a steep angle. The locomotive is from Stewart & Lloyds Pen Green shed and is 'Cardigan', a Kitson 0-6-0 built in 1934.

North Rhondda Platform, oil painting, size 10"x 14"

Glyncorrwg South pit forms the background to this atmospheric scene of a miners' special train. The colour in this painting is kept to a blending of greens, browns and yellows. The men going on shift give the painting life, and the light spreading down the valley, catching the roofs of the colliery buildings and highlighting the scene, is what caught my eye and inspired this little oil.

Steam at Holwell Works, watercolour, size 12"x 18"

Holwell Ironworks was just a stone's throw away from my home and this line and wash watercolour, painted in 2007, was done from drawings produced there in the 1960s. The engine is Stanton No.27, seen distant and dwarfed by the surrounding buildings and gantry. There is a considerable looseness of line in this painting, done to create atmosphere and drama in a scene depicting light after a storm.

The Peckett at Mountsorrel,
watercolour, size 13.5"x 9.5"

Memories of the fifties and sixties come flooding back to me, of the many hours I spent sketching and painting in the granite quarries at Mountsorrel. This single line engine shed, dilapidated and draughty, was home to the 0-6-0 tank engine 'Elizabeth'. This is a recent watercolour done in 2008 where a black ink drawing preceded the watercolour washes. It was done from a previous picture, produced on the spot in 1965. It is interesting after some forty-three years between the two to compare my techniques and results. I am pleased to say I like this one the best!

Slate at Dinorwic, watercolour, size 12"x 17.5"

The Dinorwic slate quarries in North Wales have provided me with many subjects over the years. In this scene a rather work-worn Hunslet locomotive trundles its load of slate through the quarries whose steep sides formed a dramatic setting for the picture.

This painting was commissioned from a photograph supplied to me from one of my clients, Robert Jones of Llanberis, who knew both the Dinorwic and the Penrhyn quarries very well during the years of steam operation. I envied his closeness to the location of the quarries – my own visits in the 1950s and 60s were all too few.

Steam at Oakley Quarry, watercolour, size 10.5"x 17.5"

Oakley Quarry was a great spot for observing the workings of the iron-ore industry. I did a watercolour on site sometime during the late 1960s which was not a great success but it was invaluable for its information to put this one together in 2008.

The quite dramatic outline of the quarry dwarfs both the excavation plant and the short train of wagons headed by an 0-6-0 Kitson locomotive. From the viewpoint I had for this picture the very wobbly nature of the track is quite obvious and is no exaggeration. I have seen much worse in these quarries!

Drama at Wellingborough, watercolour, size 8.5"x 11.25"

The furnaces at Wellingborough form a dramatic backdrop to this composition where a train of iron-ore wagons emerges from beneath the tunnel that carried the Midland line from London to the North. The engine is an 0-6-0 Peckett, built to run on the narrow gauge system that ran from the furnaces to the quarries further afield.

Colour at St John's Colliery, watercolour, size 17.5"x 12.5"

Engines at New Lount Colliery, watercolour, size 12"x 18"

New Lount Colliery was situated close to the Leicestershire town of Ashby-de-la-Zouch with the first of its two shafts being sunk in 1924. By the following year the company had laid down its own railway track to connect with the one-mile distant Derby-to-Ashby line of the old Midland Railway and close to the little station of Worthington.

The first of two locomotives were ordered from the Hawthorn Leslie works. The first was in 1924, later named 'George Stephenson', appropriate because the colliery's railway followed the course for part of its way to Worthington of the Coleorton railway, engineered by Stephenson in 1833. The second locomotive came along in 1929 and was named Lady Beaumont, after the Beaumont's ownership of the land and mineral rights at New Lount.

My line and wash watercolour shows both these engines, 'George Stephenson' is on the left and 'Lady Beaumont' on the right, looking well-used and towards the end of their working lives.

The colliery closed in 1968 but New Lount will forever remind me of an old friend whose association with the area went back a long way. Ashby Tilley joined an art class I was running in the early 1970s. He was then quite elderly but we soon became firm friends. Ashby's father had been the Station Master at Worthington during the latter years of the old Midland Railway's ownership of the line. We made a nostalgic trip to the area together and, sitting at Worthington, Ashby, reminisced about his boyhood days there and much about his father's life as Station Master. The day ended in him giving me the Midland Railway key his father had used to lock passengers in their carriages before departing from his care. I still have it of course and it hangs together with other relics in my railway loo at the Lazy Acre.

Twilight of an Era, watercolour, size 12"x 17.5"

In this watercolour I wanted to get across the lonely feel of these two old engines in the creeping mist of an anonymous scrapyard. I have endeavoured to paint the feeling of rust and decay – that is to say the feelings I always got on witnessing scenes like this. The picture is one of pure atmosphere and sadness for those like myself who found the steam locomotive a tremendous source of interest over the years, and as an artist a powerful inspiration to pick up my brushes and paint.

The Twilight of Steam

As a painter I have always found an attraction in subjects that show obsolescence or dereliction, rust and decay. Quite why I am not sure, except there is something in the pathos they hold, the fact that the subject has outlived its usefulness and is left to waste.

Years ago when much of Leicester was being demolished in favour of awful concrete boxes of one sort or another, I spent much of my painting time portraying deserted streets where the inner walls of what remained of a house still had its fireplaces intact, complete with wallpaper and all the evidence of a life once lived there – sometimes down to a few sticks of discarded furniture. Somebody's life uprooted and symbolised only in the remains of the moment.

The same thing is evident in some of the sketches and paintings shown here – the booking office at Lowesby and the dereliction, now gone forever, of the station architecture.

Those visits I made to the scrapyards, where the giants of the steam age awaited their turn to be cut up, provided inspirational material, emotional too because it all represented the closing of an era of technology that would leave a hole in many lives – a whole way of life for those who worked with railways throughout those years.

I suppose paintings of derelict engines or ruined stations will not perhaps appeal to some rail enthusiasts but as a painter I see such subjects on two levels. Yes, there is the pathos and the drama on the one hand, and then there are the colours involved on sometimes abstract shapes of metal where rust has taken a hold or the cutter's torch has split sections away to lie discarded in the weeds. Shapes, patterns, colours, warm against cool, hot against cold. All exciting stuff for an artist whose interests include both steam engines and architecture.

I am a great fan of the late Poet Laureate, Sir John Betjeman, who also was an enthusiast for both architecture and steam trains. I love much of his poetry and one can only be in awe of the work he did to preserve so many fine buildings from destruction, including of course St Pancras Station, where quite rightly Martin Jennings' statue to the great man can now be seen gazing towards the magnificent roof of the Barlow train shed that he felt so strongly about.

The statue perfectly captures the essence of a man whose influence and great passion for architecture saved so much from the developers. But one of the battles he unfortunately lost was that for the Euston Arch. It was an enormous blow and sadness to him that so fine a structure as the Euston Propylaeum, a great monument to the railway age, should be demolished in favour of a glass and concrete nonentity.

Betjeman was also instrumental in preserving the best of Liverpool Street Station. Together with others, his efforts prevented yet another disaster in the history of railway architecture.

Stations both great and small appealed to the poet, inspiring more than one poem that reflected his interest. But perhaps the most memorable is that of a tiny halt in the depths of rural Wiltshire whose platform is made of sleepers and where there isn't a porter, and at nightfall the guard of the last up-train put out the light! It is called 'Dilton Marsh Halt' and Sir John's prophecy in the poem, that once our roads are finally 'done for' and there is no more petrol left to burn, steam trains would return, has to a certain extent born fruit – once again steam specials do occasionally run along that stretch of line carrying their enthusiastic passengers.

The very same feelings that inspired Betjeman's poetry on the demise of the steam age and the destruction of so much of the wonderful architecture that had been so much a part of it all is what makes me want to portray those subjects in paint.

Derelict signal boxes, stations, no matter how humble; even the contents of a lineside hut, have become subjects for my brushes over the years as the steam age ground to a halt.

For me during those last few months of the steam era, when the scrapyards were full to capacity with engines awaiting demolition, my most powerful memories are of the small yard run by Cohen's at Kettering. I first went there with the late Richard Willis, who went on to be the first Chairman of the Main Line Steam Trust, now recognised as the Great Central Railway. Together with Lord Lanesborough the Trust's President, he shared a vision of what the line might one day become.

At the time, with apparently no money, the odds against anything so grand appeared to be enormous, and I confess to having been one of the many doubters, during those early stirrings of the preservation movement, that anything at all could be saved of the line and its fine buildings, let alone to see steam trains running again. Happily I was proven wrong and it is thanks to such people as Dick Willis that what we have now of the Great Central Railway is there at all.

Richard had become a friend of mine in 1968 and indeed was one of the first people to actually buy one of my railway paintings. He bought more and as a keen amateur film-maker suggested we made a film together about my painting life which we entitled 'Steam, Oil and Canvas'. We shot sequences at Tysley, Bressingham and Cohen's scrapyard at Kettering. Filming there on what were rather damp and atmospheric days inspired several paintings, two of which, produced in 1968, are reproduced here in black and white. They portray what seemed at the time to be a shortsighted waste of valuable motive power, some engines having only recently been built with years of use left in them. But the incentive on the part of the railways to gain a modern image had taken over with great urgency.

Through the mists of those few days we spent filming at Kettering, there reflected in the puddles were the jagged remains of the steam era, great abstracted chunks of a redundant technology. Nothing could more powerfully express the changes that were afoot in railway development or be a more poignant symbol of its proud and exciting past.

Richard and I found the experience of filming and painting there inspiring and so often eerie due to the mist and general atmosphere of the deserted yard. If anything totally encapsulated the twilight of steam for me as a painter of the subject, those few hours in the November of 1968 are the ones I shall always remember.

The King Awaits a Reprieve,
oil painting, size 12"x 16"

King Edward VII at Barry Docks 1971

Desolation at Cohen's Yard, oil painting, size 20"x 30", November 1968

Cylinder Block and Wheels, Cohen's Yard, Kettering, oil painting, size 24"x 36", November 1968

The Booking Office,
acrylic painting, size 5"x 5"

This little painting is a glimpse through the window of the old booking office at Lowesby in Leicestershire, on the line from Leicester to the seaside resorts of the Lincolnshire coast.

I did quite a few drawings and paintings of Lowesby in its dereliction and this one, showing the fireplace in its overgrown state surrounded by weeds, asks us to reflect on those days well gone when a ticket bought from here for one of those seaside resorts would have been, for many, a great adventure and no doubt the highlight of their year.

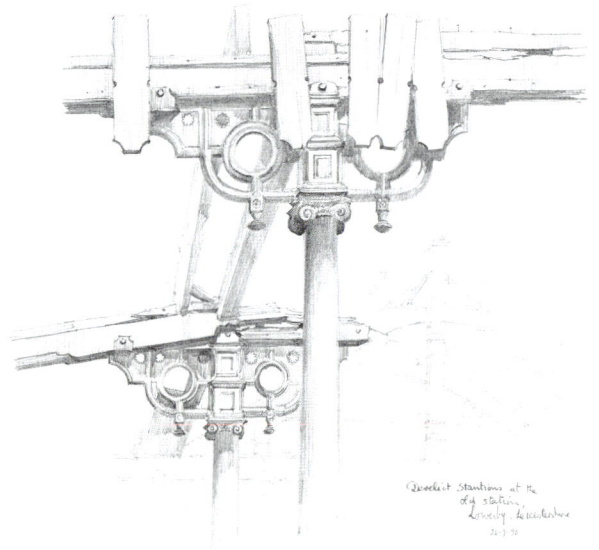

Great Northern Decline I, oil painting, size 10"x 12"

These old warehouses were on the old Great Northern Railway in Nottingham and presented a rather melancholy image on a day of changeable light. I wanted to capture in this little oil that feeling of abandon and the loneliness of the figure walking into the light. The wet track and broken-down fencing add considerably to that effect.

It is a painting that I chose to keep and it hangs in my studio.

Great Northern Decline II, watercolour, size 10"x 17"

Apart from the size and shape, this painting varies from the oil in its lighting, and of course the medium.

A strong ink line depicts the details of the architecture, and the view of the warehouses from further back includes the gate and foreground walls and pillars.

It gives an entirely different aspect of the site and a very different atmosphere, with more colour than that used in the oil.

Waiting for the Cutter's Torch, watercolour, size 12"x 19"

There was a sadness and a deserted feel to this scene at Holwell Ironworks where two of their discarded locomotives await their fate on the scrap heap.

There is an ink line used in the initial drawing of this painting, with watercolour used strongly to depict the sad state of the two engines slowly rusting away, their colour and textures being a delight to paint. I also liked the contrast between the engines and that middle-distant cauldron from the foundry, with the far-distant building and crane – the cold colour of the latter against the warmth of the foreground rusts and ochres.

Requiem for Steam, oil painting, size 12"x 16"

Evocative imagery at Holwell ironworks at the end of a winter's afternoon. The cauldron from the furnaces spoke of the run-down of the steel industry as much as those two engines did about the steam age. It may be interesting to compare this oil with the more recent watercolour 'Waiting for the Cutter's Torch', opposite, in which I used the same drawing done on the spot in the 1960s. There are obvious differences in the techniques used, but also in the shift in composition. The subject is the same but the message in each painting is very different.

Decay and Dereliction at Penrhyn, watercolour, size 13.5"x 19.5"

This very loose line and wash painting was a delight to produce and I have tried not to overstate anything within the picture, both on the engines and their surroundings. The art of understating a subject in painting is a hard one to learn as it is far too easy not to stop in good time.

The Penrhyn slate quarries, just south of Bethesda in North Wales, had a large stable of these little engines, this rather sad row having come to an end of their working lives and were slowly rusting away. On retirement one could be bought for as little as £100 and happily many were sold into preservation and still run to this day, even though many date back to being built in the 1880s.

The End of the Line, watercolour, size 7.5"x 12.5"

The old Great Central Line sank slowly into dereliction on its course through Leicester's city boundaries and in 1977 I did this watercolour only a few hundred yards from where Leicester Central Station stood. I thought I might keep it and did for a while, but my arm was twisted by one of my collectors, Rex Blaker, a Sheffield solicitor with a great passion for steam and railway architecture.

Some time later Rex died in rather tragic circumstances and his paintings were bequeathed to one of his close friends who some years later decided to sell most of the collection. I bought this one back and it now hangs in my studio to remind me of time spent on the old Great Central and also of a man whose eccentric character and company my wife and I so enjoyed.

Engines at Holwell, watercolour, size 12.5"x 18"

This watercolour depends heavily on the ink line to tell its story. I tried not to paint too much, keeping large areas with only free washes of colour over the drawn line to depict the scene.

It was a lovely subject with those two old stagers awaiting the cutter's torch and together with the surrounding plant made a dynamic composition. I regret parting with this painting, partly because of the memories I have of sketching at Holwell and partly because it is one that I have not fallen out with.

Oil Lamp and Ephemera, oil painting, size 24"x 18"

One might easily be forgiven for thinking this subject to be from some dusty old booking office in the early years of the last century. Actually it is not. It is a corner of the 'railway loo' at The Lazy Acre.

Some years ago a friend gave me a booking office 'bob-hole' glass and not knowing quite what to do with it I left it out of the way in our outside loo in the garden. But it seemed that there was not much point in having the glass without the view that might be seen through it, so I painted a wall mural of the station platforms as viewed from inside a booking office and then mounted the glass a few inches away in front of it.

It was the start of a bit of fun to decorate the whole place with a railway theme and a few bits of railwayana. The ceiling is tongue-and-groove timber with the appropriate station canopy frieze, and even the cistern is concealed within a suitcase on a pile of luggage, some with the required travel labels of course!

The photographs will give an idea of it but what cannot be deduced from them is the sound of station announcements and trains passing through that fills the place once the light is switched on. It has been great fun over the years and quite a draw at our October exhibition when from time to time I have noticed quite a queue waiting to sample its delights!

By the way, the painting of 'Oil Lamp and Ephemera' is I think, in sixty years of painting pictures, the only time that I have ever set up my easel in a lavatory.